TWAYNE'S WORLD LEADERS SERIES

Transcendentalism in America

TWLS 46

Henry David Thoreau (1856)

Ralph Waldo Emerson (*c.* 1854)   Walt Whitman (*c.* 1854)

Transcendentalism
in America

DONALD N. KOSTER

Professor of English
Adelphi University

TWAYNE PUBLISHERS
A DIVISION OF G. K. HALL & CO., BOSTON

Library of Congress Cataloging in Publication Data

Koster, Donald Nelson, 1910-
  Transcendentalism in America.

  (Twayne's world leaders series)
  Bibliography: p. 111-19.
  1. Transcendentalism (New England) I. Title.
B905.K67   191   74-20701
ISBN 0-8057-3728-8

For Rosemary

Contents

About the Author

Donald Koster received his Doctor of Philosophy degree from the University of Pennsylvania. Where he taught in the Department of English before going to Adelphi University, where he is now Professor of English and Director of the interdepartmental program in American Studies. He was for many years Bibliographer of the American Studies Association, for which he organized and directed a number of bibliographical projects that appeared in the pages of *American Quarterly*. At present he is serving as Series Editor for a series of bibliographical research guides in American Studies to be published by Gale Research Company.

Professor Koster is the author of *Divorce in the American Drama* (Univ. of Pennsylvania) as well as of numerous articles in such publications as *The American Transcendental Quarterly, American Quarterly, American Studies, The Adelphi Quarterly, The Pennsylvania Gazette,* and *American Studies: An International Newsletter*. He is also a co-author of a textbook, *Modern Journalism* (Pitman).

Professor Koster has been professionally active in the work of the American Association of University Professors, having been a chapter president at Adelphi, an organizer and first president of the Metropolitan New York Conference of AAUP, Chairman of the national Assembly of State Conferences, and member of the National Council. He is also a long-time member of the Modern Language Association and the College English Association.

Preface

Central to America's intellectual history is the Transcendental Movement. Never including any large number of participants, it nonetheless set the moral and spiritual tone for an entire generation of Americans.

Although many excellent studies of particular aspects of the Movement have been published, no broad-based study that treats it in detail has appeared since Octavius B. Frothingham's *Transcendentalism in New England* almost a century ago (1876). In the present work I have attempted to avail myself of the extensive scholarship of the past hundred years in telling the story of Transcendentalism in America as Frothingham, despite his first-hand knowledge, was unable to tell it. Not only have I tried to present the historical and philosophical background, but also I have viewed the Movement and its literary monuments with what I trust to be an unbiased critical eye. In addition I have traced in some detail the frequently subtle but distinctly persistent impact it has had on American life and letters down to the present time.

It is my hope that I have told the story in a way that will hold the interest of the reader as well as provide him with accurate and reliable information throughout. It is my further hope that my book may be useful both as an introduction to a complex subject and as a work of ready reference for the scholar in American civilization.

DONALD N. KOSTER

Garden City, New York

Chronology

1833 Frederic Hedge publishes article on Coleridge in *The Christian Examiner* (March) which provides the first American recognition of the claims of Transcendentalism.

1834 Bronson Alcott establishes his Temple School in Boston.

1835 Elizabeth Peabody publishes *Record of Mr. Alcott's School*, an account of a remarkable experiment in Transcendental education. Margaret Fuller gives her "Conversations" with "interested persons."
The Western Messenger is established in Cincinnati.

1836 Emerson publishes *Nature*.
Carlyle's *Sartor Resartus* published.
Harvard celebrates its second centennial.
The Transcendental Club is established.

1837 Emerson delivers "The American Scholar," the Phi Beta Kappa address to Harvard seniors, one of whom is Henry David Thoreau. Thoreau, responding to Emerson's suggestion, begins to keep a journal.

1838 Emerson delivers "The Divinity School Address" to graduates of Harvard Divinity School.
George Ripley publishes *Specimens of Foreign Standard Literature*.

1839 Elizabeth Peabody opens a bookshop that becomes the gathering place for Transcendentalists.
Jones Very publishes *Essays and Poems*.
James F. Clarke publishes poems in *The Western Messenger*.
Andrews Norton attacks Emerson's views in "Divinity School Address" as "the Latest Form of Infidelity."
Orestes Brownson defends Transcendentalism in the *Boston Quarterly Review* against Andrews Norton's charge of infidelity.

1840 First number of Transcendentalist organ *The Dial* published on July 1. Margaret Fuller the first editor.
Alcott's "Orphic Sayings" published in *The Dial*.

1841 Brook Farm established by George Ripley and colleagues.
Emerson's *Essays, First Series*, containing "Self-Reliance" and "The Over-Soul," published.
Theodore Parker attacks historical Christianity in his sermon "A Discourse of the Transient and Permanent in Christianity."

1842 Emerson delivers his lecture "The Transcendentalist."
Dr. William Ellery Channing dies.

1843 Bronson Alcott and friends establish Fruitlands.
William Henry Channing publishes the monthly, *The Present*, in New York. Succeeded by the *Spirit of the Age*.
The Phalanx is established. Two years later it gives way to a weekly newspaper, *The Harbinger*.
Hawthorne reveals attitude toward Transcendentalism in his allegory "The Celestial Railroad."

1844 Emerson's *Essays, Second Series* published.
Emerson delivers the lecture "New England Reformers."

1845 Margaret Fuller publishes *Woman in the Nineteenth Century*.
Thoreau moves into his cabin on Walden Pond on July 4.

1847 *The Massachusetts Quarterly Review* is established.

1848 Frederic Hedge publishes *Prose Writers of Germany*.

1849 Thoreau's essay "Resistance to Civil Government" printed in *Aesthetic Papers* edited by Elizabeth Peabody.
Thoreau's *A Week on the Concord and Merrimack Rivers* published.

1850 Margaret Fuller dies.

1851 Melville publishes *Moby Dick*.

1852 Melville publishes *Pierre*.
Hawthorne publishes *The Blithedale Romance*.

1854 *Walden* is published. Thoreau also publishes "Life Without Principle," a definition of his transcendental criticism of materialism.

1855 Whitman publishes *Leaves of Grass*.
Brownson's Quarterly Review founded.

CHAPTER 1

Definitions

A S its earliest historian, Octavius B. Frothingham, has remarked, ". . .the transcendental movement was an important factor in American life."[1] In a book notable for the enthusiasm of its commentary and the lyricism of its prose, such a
statement is conspicuous for the lowness of its key. Perhaps the
author, who described himself as once having been "a pure
Transcendentalist," wished to avoid the appearance of overstating
his case. The present writer, who does not claim to be any kind
of Transcendentalist, pure or impure, labors under no such re-
straint. He will, at the outset, declare not only that the Transcendental Movement was an important factor in American life,
but that it set the tone—intellectual, moral, and spiritual—for an
entire generation of Americans, and that its impact, although inestimable, can be felt even to the present day.

Anyone attempting to cope seriously with the task of writing
about it is faced, however, with an immediate dilemma, which is
more difficult than that of the journalist trying to define news,
the theologian God, or the poet poetry. How is one to define
Transcendentalism? Friend and foe alike have tried but none
seems to have succeeded to the complete satisfaction of anyone
but, perhaps, himself. Not that this elusive quality is to be de-
plored; it has the virtue of lending fascination to the subject.

Ralph Waldo Emerson, frequently referred to as "the spokesman of Transcendentalism," humorously spotlights this elusiveness in a letter of March 28, 1840, to his mother. He says, "You
must know I am reckoned here [Providence] a Transcendentalist, and what that beast is, all persons in Providence have a
great appetite to know: so I am carried duly about from house to
house, and all the young persons ask me, when the Lecture is
coming upon the Great Subject? . . . They have various defini-

tions of the word current here. One man, of whom I have been told, in good earnest defined it as 'Operations on the Teeth': A young man named Rodman, answered an inquiry by saying, 'It was a nickname which those who stayed behind, gave to those who went ahead.' "[2]

Nathaniel Hawthorne, by turns attracted to and repelled by the Transcendentalists and never quite certain whether he was of them or against them, echoes the strain of Emerson's letter in his story "The Celestial Railroad" when he says of a grotesque figure that appears to the traveler, "He is a German by birth, and is called Giant Transcendentalist; but as to his form, his features, his substance, and his nature generally, it is the chief peculiarity of this huge miscreant that neither he for himself, nor anybody for him, has ever been able to describe them."

Let us look, then, at some of the definitions. Frothingham calls it "a distinct philosophical system"[3] that was "essentially poetical."[4]

Frederic I. Carpenter, on the other hand, insists that American Transcendentalism was "primarily a reassertion of the mystical basis of all religion" and was therefore "primarily religious rather than philosophical."[5]

H.C. Goddard sees it as a literary movement, a philosophy and a religion all in one.[6] Walter L. Leighton calls it "the doctrine that man has a knowledge of philosophic principles by an immediate beholding without the process of reason or aid of experience."[7] It is thus subjective rather than objective as is empiricism, which claims that knowledge comes through the physical senses from experience.

Most recently Kenneth Walter Cameron, lifelong student of the subject, has attempted, it would seem, to encompass all definitions with one that describes Transcendentalism as "a warm and intuitional religious, aesthetic, philosophical and ethical movement—the American tributary of European Romanticism—a theoretical and practical way of life and a literary expression within the tradition of 'Idealism'—a new humanism based upon ancient classical or Neo-Platonic supernaturalism and colored by Oriental mysticism."[8]

It is not surprising, then, to find the prudent Emerson content to limit his definition for public consumption in his Boston lecture of 1842, "The Transcendentalist," simply to "Idealism as it appears in 1842." In the same year he was also confiding to his journal that it was "the Saturnalia of faith. It is faith run mad."[9]

That the Transcendentalists themselves disliked the name as being too ambiguous is amply borne out by their attempts to popularize such terms of self-description as the "New School" or "Disciples of the Newness." Orestes Brownson suggested "Eclecticism" as preferable to "Transcendentalism," and Bronson Alcott called the Transcendental Club, "The Symposium." But the public insisted on calling the members of the movement "Transcendentalists" and the name stuck.[10] As Hutchison has pointed out by referring to the *Dictionary of Philosophy*, edited by D.D. Runes, New York, 1942, popularly the adjective "transcendental" was attached to any philosophy thought to be "enthusiastic, mystical, extravagant, impractical, ethereal, supernatural, vague, abstruse or lacking in common sense."[11]

Christopher Pearse Cranch, that delightful caricaturist of New England Transcendentalism, himself a member of the movement, expressed the dissatisfaction best in a letter of July 11, 1840, to his father: "It is convenient to have a name which may cover all those who contend for perfect freedom, who look for progress in philosophy and theology, and who sympathize with each other in the hope that the future will not always be as the past. The name 'Transcendentalist' seems to be thus fixed upon all who profess to be on the movement side, however they may differ among themselves. . . . I prefer the term 'New School' to the other long name. This could comprehend all free seekers after truth, however their opinions differ."[12]

Typical of general public attitude is the comment of that assiduous lecturer and reader on the American Greenback circuit, Charles Dickens, who records in his *American Notes* that ". . .there has sprung up in Boston a sect of philosophers known as Transcendentalists. On inquiring what this appellation might be supposed to signify, I was given to understand that whatever was unintelligible would be certainly transcendental."

What emerges from all of the preceding is that the attempt to arrive at a watertight definition of Transcendentalism is an attempt foredoomed to failure. By comparison, catching water in a sieve would be an easy task and perhaps no more foolhardy. What all those who have tried seem to agree on is that the highly subjective, individualistic nature of the movement makes of it a many-faceted gem whose reflected light sparkles and dances with the tantalizing elusiveness of a butterfly seen in a dream within a dream. To capture it in a phrase seems impossible. Our time will perhaps be more profitably spent in attempting to examine it by describing as many of its facets as space will permit rather than in attempting to restrict it with the straitjacket of definition. We move, then, in our attempt at understanding, to an account of the origins and background of the movement.

CHAPTER 2

Major Influences

IF one were to try to pinpoint the exact time and place that
this most influential intellectual movement in American history
got under way, the trail would lead to the Reverend George Ripley's Boston study on September 19, 1836. For there Dr. Ripley,
distinguished graduate of Harvard College in 1823 and of the Divinity School in 1826, for ten years minister of the new Unitarian
Church in Purchase Street, and a recognized leader of the liberal
wing of Unitarianism, called together a group of his friends, including A. Bronson Alcott, Orestes A. Brownson, Ralph Waldo
Emerson, Frederic Henry Hedge, Convers Francis and James
Freeman Clarke, in order "to see how far it would be possible for
earnest minds to meet." Unitarians all, they were dissatisfied with
Unitarianism's lack of a positive approach to life and religion and
believed that the time had come to give expression to a new and
vital faith. The Transcendental Movement was the result.

Of course, the seedbed had been sown for Transcendentalism
many years before. The influences are many and they are varied,
with scholars in considerable disagreement as to their number
and degree of importance. It is, however, possible to enumerate
those that inescapably played a role. They are Platonism,
Puritanism, Romanticism, and Orientalism.

Central to the Platonic philosophy is the idea of the Supreme
Good as primary, with all things deriving from it. Thus a duality
is established, with the Supreme Good, synonymous with reason,
on the one hand, and all else, which we may call matter, on the
other. The good life is a progress away from the transient many
to the permanent One, the Supreme Good.

The Transcendentalists were, however, more closely allied with
Neoplatonic thinking than with Platonic. For Neoplatonism suggests the intuitive certainty that the highest good lies beyond

empirical experience, leading to the conviction that all earthly
things are vain. For Plotinus the idea of the One, the Primeval
Being, as beyond time, space, thought, reason, is paramount.
Without attributes, it is the source of all things, including the
ideal world. His insight to truth comes more through mystic vision than through the dialectical reasoning characteristic of Plato,
and thus he is closer kin to the Transcendentalists. One of his
most important original contributions is the idea of ecstasy, the
mystic union of the human soul with God. Rising above all
things, it may merge with the Primal Being itself. This ecstasy is
felt only by some men, but seldom at best. One is reminded of
Emerson's description in *Nature* of the ecstasy that made him
"glad to the brink of fear."

Since the Transcendentalists were, with few exceptions, pro-
ducts of an educational system that stressed the study of the clas-
sics, their acquaintance with Plato and the Neoplatonists cannot
be seriously questioned. Harrison, for example, has demonstrated
in his *The Teachers of Emerson*, Emerson's intensive reading of
this literature. And in this regard Emerson was but one among
many.

As for the influence of Puritanism, it is rooted in the inescapa-
ble fact that the Transcendentalists were, almost to a man, the
direct descendants of those who had come to New England in
pursuit of the impossible dream of establishing the Kingdom of
God on earth. Their ethical idealism owes more than most of
them would ever have admitted to their Calvinistic legacy. For,
as Hutchison has pointed out, American Congregational churches
from the middle of the seventeenth century were based on
Genevan Calvinism as interpreted by English churchmen of the
Cromwellian era.[1] This interpretation centered on the ideas of
the absolute sovereignty of God, so brilliantly defended by
Jonathan Edwards in his *Personal Narrative*, the revelation of
God in the Trinity, the final authority of Scripture for human
faith and action, the divine decision made prior to the Creation
whether to elect particular men to salvation or condemn them to
eternal damnation, and the inability of those chosen for salvation
to refuse it or to behave in a manner that would cause it to be
withdrawn. Thus it follows, as Santayana observed in his famous
lecture, "The Genteel Tradition in American Philosophy," that
Calvinism asserted strenuously "that sin exists, that sin is

punished, and that it is beautiful that sin should exist to be punished." But this bleak doctrine that man is conceived in sin, born in sin, and lives in sin was challenged strenuously by the dawn rays of the Enlightenment, which began to recognize the innate goodness of man as a divinely created organism reflecting the goodness of its maker.

As Goddard has made clear, the background that made Transcendentalism possible in New England is the history of the revolt against Calvinism that took shape in the rise of Unitarianism.[2] Grounded in deistic rationalism, it was able to attack Calvinism with cold logic. Attempting to reconcile science with religion, the deists had accepted the authority of human reason as John Locke had explained it, rejected the miraculous, and denied not only the Trinity but also the divinity of Jesus and the authority of the Bible as the unquestionable word of God. Nominally, the Unitarian dissent from Congregationalism was over the doctrine of the Trinity; but realistically, it was over the nature of man and his ability to contribute to his own salvation.[3] Central to the Unitarians' creed was its doctrine of human nature rather than its doctrine of God.[4] Man, they held, possessed an infinite capacity for good, of which Jesus, a man rather than a God, was a prime exemplar.

So appealing was this doctrine to a people who had willingly embraced the Puritan view that it was in keeping with God's will for man to amass material possessions but who were increasingly reluctant to accept the other side of the coin, predestination, that by 1785 King's Chapel, the Anglican church in Boston, became openly Unitarian, and by 1815 fourteen of the sixteen pre-Revolutionary Boston Congregational churches had followed suit. Boston Unitarianism may then quite properly be called, to use Stephen Whicher's phrase, the marriage of New England Puritanism and the Enlightenment.[5]

But the thirty-year feud with New England Calvinism was scarcely over before the "Unitarian Controversy," as it came to be called, erupted. Inspired at least in part by Dr. William Ellery Channing, minister of the Federal Street Church from 1803 until 1842, and leading spirit of Boston Unitarianism, a group of younger ministers determined to free the church from what Emerson was to call its "pale negations." Channing, increasingly impatient with the smugness, the rationalistic approach and the lack of moral fervor of the church he had embraced, formulated in 1819 in his sermon "Unitarian Christianity" the classic statement of the liberal creed. Its call for a more active faith provided the necessary spark for the Transcendental revolt. Not that Channing himself could ever accept what he came to regard as the excesses of his young friends, many of them his former students at Harvard; he stopped short of being a Transcendentalist. But it was he who fanned the Transcendental spirit into a flame, a spirit that Goddard has likened to the French Revolutionary spirit that distrusted the past, was optimistic about the future, and was confident of solving the problems of mankind.[6] But Goddard also sees the Transcendentalists who set out initially to reform the Unitarian church and ended, in many instances, by breaking with it altogether, as "Puritans to the core." Indeed, this Puritanism he views as the "signally American contribution to transcendentalism."[7] Sincerity, purity, moral courage, unselfish adherence to an ideal—these are qualities that reflected the better side of Puritanism. And surely men like Emerson, Alcott, Thoreau, and Parker possessed them in full measure.

Transcendentalism has frequently been viewed, as by Merle Curti, as part of the larger romantic movement. "It was," he writes, "a revolt against the rationalism of the 18th Century. It emphasized those aspects of man's nature that were said to transcend or be independent of experience."[8] And what were the hallmarks of the romantic movement? The delight in, and wonder at, the beauty and beneficence of nature, the recognition of the individual human being as superior to society, the concomitant objection to social restraints upon the individual, and, above all, the ascendancy of emotion and intuitive perception over reason. Faith becomes the primary source of knowledge, and the creativity of man is stressed.

Such German romanticists as Goethe, Herder, and Kant held that experience is much broader than the reason of the Enlightenment; consequently they encouraged a reaction against the empiricism of Locke and the skepticism of Hume. The philosophical high-water mark of their revolt against the rationalists was Immanuel Kant's brilliant *Critique of Pure Reason.*

It was Kant who first employed the word "transcendental" as it was to be applied in nineteenth century usage. And, as Hutchi-

son notes, the transcendental philosophy that he proposed in the
Critique was a systematic exposition of the nature of a priori
knowledge.[9] Such concepts as space and time are natural to the
human mind, he held, and are therefore logically prior to the experience of the physical senses. Central to this thesis is the idea
that the mind is endowed with elemental concepts and forms of
intuition that could not be derived through induction but which
are necessary to a reliable knowledge of the phenomenological
world. Most important to the American transcendentalists, Kant,
in Frothingham's excellent analysis,

asserted the veracity of consciousness, and demanded an absolute ac-
knowledgment of that veracity. The fidelity of the mind to itself was a first
principle with him. Having these ideas, of the soul, of God, of a moral
law; being certain that they neither originated in experience, nor depended on experience for their validity, that they transcended experience altogether—man was committed to an unswerving and uncom-
promising loyalty to himself. His prime duty consisted in deference to
the integrity of his own mind. The laws of his intellectual and moral nature were inviolable.[10]

In his chapter "Transcendentalism in Germany" Frothingham,
after his exposition of Kant's work, admirably sums up the succes-
sive contributions of Jacobi, Fichte, and Schelling and suggests
that "the idealists of New England were largest debtors to Jacobi
and Fichte."[11] Using Frothingham's exact words, Curti views
American Transcendentalism, then, as "spiritual and practical
rather than metaphysical."[12]

The question of whether German romantic thought came to
America through the return of enthusiastic American students
like Edward Everett, George Ticknor, and George Bancroft or
through the interpretations of English romanticists like Coleridge,
Wordsworth, and Carlyle or through a more general transatlantic
passage of ideas is still a moot point, with scholars to be found on
virtually every side of the issue. René Wellek, for example, has
been at some pains to explode the first two suggestions,[13] contending that Everett had no interest in it and even Ticknor and
Bancroft were scarcely absorbed in German philosophy. Frederic
Henry Hedge he finds to be the single exception. Whatever the
reality may have been, the fact is that not only German romantic
philosophy but the French eclectic school, especially Victor

Cousin and Theodore Jouffroy, became influential in shaping American Transcendental thought. The principal difference between the French and German post-Kantian romantic philosophers resides in the Frenchmen's emphasis on validating, by psychological and historical analysis, the truths provided by intuition.

For many Americans, however, at least in the earlier stages of the Transcendental Movement, the romantic philosophy came most easily by way of Coleridge, Carlyle, and Wordsworth. Coleridge, who had lived and studied in Germany, was most influential with his distinction between the Understanding and the Reason, a distinction that Emerson was to invoke in *Nature*. Briefly stated, Understanding is equated with Science or Knowing, Reason with Wisdom, a revelation that comes only through deep feeling or intuition.

Carlyle, coming to German philosophy mainly through German literature, provided tremendous stimulus to American Transcendentalism with his *Sartor Resartus*, which Emerson in his enthusiasm had published in the United States after Carlyle had vainly sought a British publisher. As Tony Tanner has observed, "three of Emerson's key ideas received tremendous impetus from Carlyle's work."[14] They are the need for an attitude of wonder in viewing nature; a conviction that every object, even the smallest, is a symbol of God; and a rejection of history in favor of "the everlasting NOW."

Primary in Wordsworth's appeal to the Transcendentalists was his romantic belief that childhood is "a visionary state to which man should attempt to return."[15] The child in his uneducated state is endowed with a feeling of the organic wholeness of the universe, with a natural capacity for wonder and delight that is enfeebled by the intellectual activity of logical analysis that comes with education in the social state. This emphasis upon the child of nature as the only true philosopher is echoed again and again in the literature of the American Transcendentalists, with Emerson and Whitman its most brilliant expositors.

The final major influence on Transcendentalism in America is the Oriental. Arthur Christy, whose book *The Orient in American Transcendentalism* remains the preeminent study of the subject, has provided convincing evidence that American interest in the Orient, which began with the China trade so profitably engaged in by numerous New England merchants, turned from the merely economic to the spiritual and moral, and that this change coincided with the growth of the Transcendental Movement. He sees Emerson, for example, as preoccupied with Oriental thought and possessing temperamental affinities with it despite taking only what he wanted and borrowing only some forms of expression from it.[16] As for Thoreau, he believes that he gained his enthusiasm for Oriental literature from Emerson, particularly during the year of 1841 that he spent living in Emerson's home and reading Emerson's books.[17] How the third great American Transcendentalist writer, Walt Whitman, became interested in Oriental philosophy is less clear, but even a cursory reading of *Leaves of Grass* reveals its impact on the poet. Indeed Carpenter goes so far as to express the conviction that Emerson, Thoreau, and Whitman started a movement toward Orientalism that expanded rapidly in American literature.[18] But Carpenter also makes the important point that Emerson remained Occidental while reinterpreting the Oriental books.[19] Indeed Washburn remarks with much justification that "Emerson and the Transcendentalists, despite their rapturous praise of the wisdom of the East, actually misconceived or ignored its underlying meaning."[20] He shows that the Transcendentalists were "the first group in the United States to seize upon and popularize the translations of Oriental works which were just then coming from the pens of European scholars. The Vedas, the Upanishads, the Mahabharata, the Code of Manu, Buddha, Confucius, Mencius, the Koran, the Persian poets, all passed before their eyes and received their enraptured praise."[21] He sees them, however, as taking the Oriental ideas out of context and frequently misinterpreting them. "Why, then," he asks,

did the Transcendentalists consider their thought to have such a close affinity to Oriental thought? The answer to this question seems to be that they were carried away by the realization that so many of the doctrines which they considered so radically daring had been comprehended thousands of years before by civilizations which they had always conceived of as inferior if not barbaric. In the first flush of recognition, these New Englanders seized the outwardly similar statements of these doctrines without understanding or caring to understand that they did not represent at bottom thought that was at all similar to theirs. They tried to take the wisdom of a sad view of temporal existence and use it to confirm their own 'joyful' view of life.[22]

The reply that Emerson and the other Transcendentalists might well have made to such a charge is contained in "The American Scholar," in which Emerson insists that books "are for nothing but to inspire. I had better never see a book than to be warped by its attraction clean out of my own orbit, and made a satellite instead of a system."[23]

It is, perhaps, worth noting that such a careful student of Emerson's inner self as Stephen Whicher believes that what Emerson felt Asia had primarily to teach him was "the universal identity of things, their unity in Brahma, before which all notion of individual freedom vanishes. . . ," but that he came to this view no earlier than 1845, after which the many references in his journal indicate the strong influence of Oriental thought.[24]

Regardless of the degree of importance of any of the influences sketched in the foregoing pages, the vital fact to remember is that the young men and women who created the Transcendental Movement were self-proclaimed radicals and mystics. In the words of Van Wyck Brooks:

the more sensitive minds of the younger generation, the imaginative, the impressionable, the perceptive, . . .were thoroughly disaffected. The shape of the outward world had ceased to please them. The Fourth of July orations had ceased to convince them that "freedom" had any connection with freedom of mind or that "liberality" in religion had any connection with religious feeling. . . . They had no interest in size, numbers and dollars. They had begun to explore the inner life, the depths of thought and sentiment. They had returned, on another level, to the mental habits of their Pilgrim forbears.[25]

CHAPTER 3

The Transcendental Club,
Brook Farm and Fruitlands,
The Movement in the West

W E return now to the Boston study of Dr. Ripley on the af-
ternoon of September 19, 1836. In attendance, as we have
seen, were his friends Emerson, Alcott, Hedge, Francis, Clarke,
and Brownson. Recording the meeting in his journal, Emerson
notes that "the conversation was earnest and hopeful. It inspired
hope."[1] The session seems to have been, however, primarily a
business meeting, at which it was agreed that the first genuine
discussion should be held at Alcott's house at 3 P.M. on October
3, on the topic "American Genius—the Causes which Hinder Its
Growth, Giving Us no First-Rate Productions."[2] The topic had
obviously grown out of Emerson's remark at the preliminary
meeting that there was not one unchallengeable reputation among
American artists, citing Washington Allston, the painter; Bryant,
the poet; Horatio Greenough, the sculptor; and Dr. Channing to
illustrate his point.[3]

Emerson tells us also that a rule was suggested for the new
club that no one would be admitted whose presence would ex-
clude the discussion of any topic.[4]

The original members were an impressive if youthful group.
Francis at forty was the oldest, Clarke at twenty-six the youngest.
The others were in their thirties. All were of scholarly bent, with
Hedge already having established something of a reputation with
his knowledge of German thought and literature, eventually to
blossom into the publication in 1848 of his *Prose Writers of Germany*, Ripley being well known as a writer on foreign philosophy
for *The Christian Examiner*, and Brownson having achieved at

least local renown for his skill in controversy. Emerson himself had, only two weeks earlier, seen his own first volume, *Nature*, placed before the public, a volume that, as Rusk has observed, "would have served better than any other as the manifesto of the Transcendentalists."[5]

Meetings of the club, which became known variously by the members as the Symposium or Hedge's Club (because on Hedge's removal to Bangor, Maine, meetings tended to be held whenever he could make a trip back to Boston) but by the public as the Transcendental Club (the name that has stuck), were held four or five times a year for about four years with a considerable coming and going of personnel. The "regulars" in attendance were Emerson; Alcott; Henry Thoreau; Caleb Stetson; George and Sophia Ripley; Mrs. Samuel Ripley, whom Rusk has called "a human mill, grinding German, Italian, Greek, chemistry, metaphysics, or theology, utterly indifferent as to which was thrown into her hopper";[6] John S. Dwight, later to be the dictator of Boston's taste in music; Margaret Fuller, impetuous high priestess of the Movement; Elizabeth Peabody, who, with Margaret, assisted Bronson Alcott in his educational experiment at the Temple School in Boston; the indefatigable Theodore Parker, who was to succeed Emerson as the acknowledged leader of the Movement; the Plymouth tutor, Robert Bartlett; Jones Very, who believed his poems to be directly dictated by God; Convers Francis; John Weiss; the Rev. Cyrus A. Bartol; and Hedge.

Others who were associated with the club and attended now and then were the Rev. David Hatch Barlow, a minister in Lynn and then in Worcester; George P. Bradford, brilliant scholar and descendant of Governor Bradford; Ephraim Peabody, minister of the Federal Street Church in Boston; Chandler Robbins, who succeeded Emerson at the Second Church in Boston; the Rev. George Ware Briggs of Plymouth; George Putnam, minister of the First Church in Roxbury; Samuel Osgood; Thomas T. Stone; the brothers Channing; the abolitionist agitator Samuel J. May; Christopher P. Cranch; George Bancroft; Clevenger the sculptor; Samuel G. Ward, a literary Bostonian; William Russell; Sophia Peabody, and her husband-to-be, Nathaniel Hawthorne.[7] But record-keeping was casual, organization was minimal, and informality was the order of the day in this group of the "like-minded" who were about as stubbornly individualistic as any group of persons could possibly be. What it did provide was a forum in which ideas could be explored, reactions noted, and encouragement provided. The earlier discussions were theological as might be expected in a group whose members were or had been ministers. Revelation, inspiration, providence, law, and truth were among the topics openly treated. If the members exhibited any tendency in common in their discussions, it was a pantheistic view of life.[8]

One should not, however, deduce from the seemingly passive nature of the Transcendental Club that its members were parlor radicals. They were far from satisfied to be theoretical metaphysicians or mystics oblivious of the world about them. As Emerson was to indicate in "The American Scholar," action, though it may be subordinate with the scholar, is essential. "Without it thought can never ripen into truth."[9] And these were primarily preachers who had to live and translate their philosophy into practice. This they did not only through their sermons, but through schools, conversations, lecturing, the writing of essays, and participation in reform movements. They did not intend, in the words of Odell Shepard, that the "capitalists, merchants, engineers, politicians and scientists who had lost their minds in developing their brains" should run away with America.[10]

No doubt about it, the forces of material progress were in the saddle and riding hard. The rising industrial order of the North allied with the slave-holding, cotton-growing South was creating waves of prosperity that threatened to engulf the nation in a tide of aimless physical growth cloaked in the Doctrine of Progress. Everything that contributed to this prosperity—slavery, the exploitation of "free" labor, massacres of the Indians, the rape of the forests, the Mexican War—was defended in the name of progress. Indeed, the Doctrine of Progress was invoked "to give a cloak of idealism to what was more bluntly called manifest destiny."[11] The Transcendentalists were as one in feeling that their country was advancing rapidly in exactly the wrong direction. It was not that they were opposed to the idea of progress; far from it. But progress was not truly progress unless it was directed aright. And what was the right direction? As Ekirch clearly puts it, "In the minds of Emerson and the Transcendentalists, the progress of society depended primarily upon the improvement of its individual members."[12] Mind, then, must gain the ascendancy over matter.

Although in its philosophic form the message of the Transcendentalists made small immediate appeal to the masses of the American public, its thrust as Curti has outlined it, was true to the spirit of genuine democracy:

1. The exaltation of man, all men.
2. The idea that all power and wisdom come from nature, with which man must form a firsthand relationship.
3. The relegation of books to a secondary place in the scale of values.
4. The insistence that instinct is good and must be obeyed rather than curbed by convention and authority.

Indeed, the seeking, the glorification of the individual, the social sympathies of the Transcendentalists corresponded to the democratic doctrine that all men possess a sacred right to govern themselves and to reach for the stars.[13]

Odell Shepard's observation that "Transcendentalism was in essence a philosophy and a religion of reform"[14] is indubitably true. Indeed, Ekirch sees it as the popular reform philosophy of the 1840's.[15] Even public figures like Abe Lincoln in Illinois caught the spirit of the times in looking forward to the happy day when mind would subdue passion, conquer matter, control the appetites, and rule the world. Of course, reform movements were virtually in the very atmosphere throughout the era: vegetarianism, women's rights, temperance, Sabbath reform, nonresistance, spiritualism, abolition, perfectionism were but some that vied for popular attention. But Transcendentalism had a broader base than any of them and attracted to its banner many young Americans who were seeking a way to broaden their intellectual and spiritual horizons in order to realize their human potential. Indeed it appealed to many because it seemed to be a path toward discovering the reality of self. Emerson perhaps put it best when he confided to his journal in 1843, "the Transcendentalist or Realist is distinguished from the churchman herein, that he limits his affirmation to his simple perception, and never goes beyond the warrant of his experience (spiritual and sensuous) in his creed, whilst the churchman affirms many things as received on testimony as of equal value with the moral intuitions."[16]

The Transcendentalists, however, were no more united in their views of reform than they were in anything else. In fact, they divided into two quite distinct camps. On the one hand were those who sought to advance their views by acting within established social groups or by forming new ones. On the other were those who remained aloof from social efforts and chose to reform and to teach through example and through art. For them the individualistic rather than the social aspects of Transcendentalism were important. Emerson and Thoreau would be prime exemplars of those who chose to test the inner life to its fullest and report their discoveries in their writings. The individualists held that, if the Transcendentalist premises were true, they would transform the inner man. Reform, in other words, must take place within the living soul.

The most widely known of the experiments in social reform was undoubtedly Brook Farm. The leading spirit in this enterprise was Dr. Ripley, who, with his wife, Sophia, had spent part of the summer of 1840 as a visitor at the farm, then owned by the Ellis family. Situated on the borders of Newton, West Roxbury, and Dedham, it was by all accounts a beautiful place. In the winter of that year Ripley decided to purchase the property from the Ellises. To raise the necessary $30,000, he proposed to form a joint stock company with shares to be sold at $500. When the Articles of Association of the Subscribers to the Brook Farm Institute of Agriculture and Education were executed on September 29, 1841, there were ten subscribers, who among them had pledged $12,000. They included Ripley and his wife, Charles A. Dana, a recent graduate of Harvard and later to win fame as editor of the New York *Sun*, and Nathaniel Hawthorne, who was in search of a comfortable place in which to settle with his wife-to-be, Sophia Peabody. On October 11, 1841, the deed transferring ownership to the Association was signed, and this most famous of Transcendentalist communities became an official reality. Article II stated the object of the Association thus: "to purchase such estates as may be required for the establishment and continuance of an agricultural, literary, and scientific school or college, to provide such lands and houses, animals, libraries and apparatus, as may be found expedient or advantageous to the main purpose of the Association."[17]

On October 30 the members voted to charge $4.00 per week for board, including house-rent, fuel, light, and washing. Board, however, would be free in proportion to the time a member employed in behalf of the Association: one year's board for one year's labor; one half year's board for one half year's labor, and so on, with three hundred days' labor being considered equal to one year's; with the work week being sixty hours from May through September, forty-eight from October through April.[18]

Shares continued to sell, and by the end of six years there were over a hundred and forty associates.[19] To the central building, which went by the appropriate name of the Hive, were added the Eyrie, the Cottage, and the Pilgrim House.

The members were, for the most part, young, and none was old. As with youth of the present generation, beards and long hair were in favor with the men, loose flowing hair with the women.

Emerson, in his one hundredth lecture before the Concord Lyceum in 1880, remembers these young people thus:

Those who inspired and organized it [Brook Farm] were of course persons impatient of the routine, the uniformity, perhaps they would say the squalid contentment of society around them, which was so timid and skeptical of any progress. One would say then that impulse was the rule in the society, without centripetal balance; perhaps it would not be severe to say, intellectual *sansculottism,* an impatience of the formal, routinary character of our educational, religious, social and economical life in Massachusetts. Yet there was immense hope in these young people.[20]

But Emerson, despite his sympathies with the Brook Farmers, refused to join them. His journal entries of the time record that he suspected it was folly to bring "the good and like-minded together into families, into a colony." He preferred that they disperse "and so leaven the whole lump of society." On October 16, 1840, Dr. and Mrs. Ripley, Margaret Fuller, and Bronson Alcott met with him and discussed Ripley's plan. He wished, he says, "to be convinced, to be thawed, to be made nobly mad by the kindlings before my eye of a new dawn of human piety . . . not once could I be inflamed, but sat aloof and thoughtless; my voice faltered and fell. . . . I do not wish to remove from my present prison to a prison a little larger. I wish to break all prisons. . . . Moreover, to join this body would be to traverse all my long trumpeted theory, and the instinct which spoke from it, that one man is a counterpoise to a city—that a man is stronger than a city, that his solitude is more prevalent and beneficent than the concert of crowds."[21]

Ripley, who wrote to Emerson on November 9, 1840, urging him again to join, explained his dream succinctly: "I wish," he said, "to see a society of educated friends, working, thinking, and living together, with no strife, except that of each to contribute the most to the benefit of all."[22]

Emerson announced his decision in a letter to Ripley of December 15, 1840. While extolling Ripley's design as "noble and humane," he explains that all he shall solidly do, he must do alone. "If the community is not good for me neither am I good for it. I do not look on myself as a valuable member to any community which is not either very large or very small and select."[23]

In general, the more self-sufficient of the Transcendentalists concurred with Emerson. They were willing to lend encouragement, time, and even money to the Brook Farm enterprise, but they refused to join. Among the better known visitors besides Emerson were Margaret Fuller, William Henry Channing, Bronson Alcott, the English mystic Charles Lane, Christopher Cranch, Orestes Brownson, Elizabeth Peabody, Albert Brisbane, the Fourierist, and Horace Greeley. Indeed Emerson often came to lead the talk, and Miss Fuller even conducted a Conversation on Education for the Farmers. Only Henry Thoreau remained entirely aloof. Although he was apparently invited to join, his response goes unrecorded except for the typically acid comment in his journal: "As for these communities, I think I had rather keep bachelor's hall in hell than go to board in heaven."[24]

Nor did all of the members find Brook Farm the haven they had hoped for. Most famous of the disgruntled was Hawthorne, who had in the beginning been persuaded by Ripley's argument that if creative artists would pool their resources they could, with a few hours' physical labor each day, have a larger freedom for their creative activity. But Hawthorne's enthusiasm quickly waned as he saw that some members shirked their share of the labor, leaving the more conscientious to pick up the slack. His journal comment is devastating: "Even my Custom-House experience was not such a thraldom and weariness; my mind and heart were freer."[25] And in his novel *The Blithedale Romance* he was to portray Brook Farm in such an unflattering light that even Emerson could not forgive him.

Although Hawthorne seemed to feel that the Association

tended to stifle individual freedom, Charles Lane in *The Dial* criticized it for being too individualistic. Said he, "It is not a community; it is not truly an association; it is merely an aggregation of persons, and lacks that oneness of spirit which is probably needful to make it of help and lasting value to mankind."[26]

As the Articles of Association indicate, education was to be the main purpose of the Association. The educational policy, as summarized by Swift, was one of "perfect freedom of intercourse between students and a teaching body of men and women whose moral attainments were not distanced by their mental accomplishments. . . ."[27] And the Brook Farm school was a very good one. Ripley taught philosophy and mathematics, Mrs. Ripley history and Italian. Charles A. Dana held classes in Greek and German, while Dwight taught music. Botany and geology were studied by means of "field work." No course of study was compulsory; each student was free to follow what attracted him.

After more than two years as a purely voluntary and private association, Brook Farm succumbed to the pressures of the Fourierists, notably Horace Greeley and Albert Brisbane, who wished to see it become a phalanstery where the social philosophy of the revered Fourier could be applied. Partly under the pressure of strained finances, the Farmers went along, changed their Articles of Association into a modified Fourierist Constitution, and lost the unique character of the Farm. Swift goes so far as to say that "the attempt to transform Brook Farm into a modified Fourierist Phalanx proved its ruin."[28] The building of a great central community house to be called the Phalanstery was begun in the summer of 1844. An assembly hall, a dining room for more than 300, a reading room, reception rooms, and single rooms and suites for families were to be included, along with a kitchen and bakery. Built of wood, it was to be 175 feet long.[29] In March of 1846 a fire broke out in the nearly completed structure, entirely consuming it, and with it the dream of Brook Farm. Not yet insured, the vast building was a total loss, and the days of the community were numbered. By the summer of 1847 a meeting of the Brook Farm Phalanx's stockholders and creditors voted to transfer the property to a Board of three Trustees "for the purpose of disposing of it to the best advantage of all concerned."[30]

Almost all of those who participated in the life of the Farm who have written about it—and they were many—remembered the experience affectionately. Perhaps Emerson, who was not of them but for them, summed up their experience best. "What knowledge," he said,

of themselves and of each other, what various practical wisdom, what personal power, what studies of character, what accumulated culture many of the members owed to it! What mutual measure they took of each other! It was a close union, like that in a ship's cabin, of clergymen, young collegians, merchants, mechanics, farmers' sons and daughters, with men and women of rare opportunities and delicate culture, yet assembled there by a sentiment which all shared . . . of the honesty of a life of labor and of the beauty of a life of humanity.[31]

The other Transcendentalist experiment in communal living was Bronson Alcott's Fruitlands. Brook Farm had not been austere enough to suit Alcott, who did not believe in domesticating animals to be slaves to man or in eating the flesh of animals, our fellow beings. In a letter of February 15, 1843, to Isaac T. Hecker, one of the Brook Farmers who was later to convert to Roman Catholicism and to found the Paulist order, he laid out the purposes of Fruitlands. "First," he said, "to obtain the free use of a spot of land adequate by our own labor to our support; including, of course, a convenient plain house, and offices, wood-lot, garden, and orchard.

"Second, to live independently of foreign aids by being sufficiently elevated to procure all articles for subsistence in the productions of the spot, under a regimen of healthful labor and recreation; with benignity toward all creatures, human and inferior, with beauty and refinement in all economics; and the purest charity throughout our demeanor."[32]

Alcott's English friend, Charles Lane, purchased the Wyman farm at Harvard, Massachusetts, in 1843, and in June of that year with his son, William, he joined Alcott, his wife and four daughters there, along with H. C. Wright, another of Alcott's English disciples, Isaac Hecker, Samuel Bower, Christopher Greene, Samuel Larned, Abraham Everett, Anna Page, Joseph Palmer, and Abram Wood.

Life was difficult from the start. Because no animal substance—flesh, fish, butter, cheese, eggs, or milk—could be used since they were denounced as pollution tending to corrupt the body and through it the soul, the diet was meager. Tea, coffee, molasses, and rice were also proscribed—the latter two as foreign luxuries—and only water was used as a beverage. Besides their refusal to eat meat or use the labor of animals, they would not use animal manure as fertilizer (because this was seen as an unjust forcing of nature) or wear woolen clothes. Nor would they wear cotton because slaves were used in its production. Thus they garbed themselves in linen tunics and wore canvas shoes. Even their vegetarianism was strained because they would eat no vegetable that showed its lower nature by growing downward like the beet, the carrot, or the potato. Only those that grew heavenward, such as corn, beans, and melons, were acceptable. Since the farm's soil was none too rich to begin with, the Fruitlands table scarcely groaned under the weight of the obtainable approved fare. But outward abstinence was viewed as a sign of inward fullness as Lane and Alcott declared.

Elevated conversation and high thinking failed to save the little colony from the onset of a savage New England winter. The meager diet generated insufficient heat to keep bodies garbed only in linen tunics from shivering in the icy blasts that penetrated every crack of the ancient farmhouse, and before December was out, the blithe spirits of June had become wraiths obliged to flee to the warmer hearths of more conventional society. Years later, Louisa May Alcott was to write a delightfully satiric yet nostalgic reminiscence of those seven months at Fruitlands called "Transcendental Wild Oats." Shining through the satire and the nostalgia is an earnest paragraph that sums up Bronson Alcott and his noble aspirations—as well as those of other dedicated Transcendentalists—better than anyone else has yet done.

He had tried, but it was a failure. The world was not ready for Utopia yet, and those who attempted to found it only got laughed at for their pains. In other days, men could sell all and give to the poor, lead lives devoted to holiness and high thought, and, after the persecution was over, find themselves honored as saints or martyrs. But in modern times these things are out of fashion. To live for one's principles, at all costs, is a dangerous speculation, and the failure of an ideal, no matter how humane and noble, is harder for the world to forgive and forget than bank robbery or the grand swindles of corrupt politicians.[33]

Alcott, though bent by the failure of the noble experiment,

was not broken. He had other strings to his bow as we shall see in a subsequent chapter.

Despite the forays into institutional living, the New England Transcendentalists remained for the most part strongly individualistic, preferring the idea of reform of the self as a mode of reforming society to the idea of reforming institutions. In his journal Emerson speaks of a talk he had in 1842, at the zenith of the Brook Farm experiment, with Edmund Hosmer:

We talked of G. R. and his project. I cannot help feeling a profound compassion for G.R. & S.R. [George Ripley and Sophia Ripley] who by their position are or must be inevitably, one would say, transformed into charlatans, by the endeavor continually to meet the expectation & admiration of all this eager crowd of men & women seeking they know not what who flock to them. . . .

Friendship, fine people; yes; Association & grand phalanx of the best of the human race; the best, banded for some transcendent project; O yes; Excellent; but remember, that nothing & no society can ever be so large as one man. . . . the first hour in which he mortgages himself to two or ten or twenty . . . he dwarfs himself below the stature of one.[34]

Had they had Emerson's gift for incisive expression, most of those in New England who considered themselves Transcendentalists would have said the same thing.

But Transcendentalism was not confined to New England. It made its way to the Midwest in the wagons of emigrants from New England who were in search of richer land and broader opportunities than the Eastern seaboard offered them. Paul R. Anderson has shown conclusively the importance of the New England writers in influencing the western brand of Transcendental thought. For example, in 1835 in Cincinnati, James Freeman Clarke, William G. Eliot and Ephraim Peabody established *The Western Messenger*, a journal whose stated purpose was "to set forth and defend Unitarian views of Christianity,"[35] which, in light of its founders, meant Transcendental views. As Gohdes notes, the content of *The Messenger* was strikingly similar to that of *The Dial*, with many of the same people contributing. Then there were the numerous trips west made by Emerson and Alcott,[36] which began in 1850 with Emerson's accepting the invitation of a Cincinnati group to address them.

Transcendentalism in the Midwest may be said to have crested with the St. Louis Movement, which Pochmann has shown to have had a close relation to New England Transcendentalism in philosophy, literature, and education.[37] Harmon, however, emphasizes that the St. Louis Movement was also "a reaction against both New England transcendentalism and the materialistic school exemplified in Herbert Spencer."[38] She sees it as feeling a need for a social philosophy aimed at showing man how "to achieve freedom within his society" rather than rejecting, in the New England way, intellectual formalism and normal social institutions on the ground that the individual should discover his deepest insights for himself.[39]

Three quite remarkable individuals formed the core of the St. Louis Movement. They were Henry C. Brokmeyer, William Torrey Harris, and Denton J. Snider. Brokmeyer, born in Germany, came to America as a youth, worked as a day laborer but eventually became Lt. Governor of Missouri (1876–80). Harris taught in the St. Louis schools, became a principal and superintendent, and in 1889 U.S. Commissioner of Education. Snider, who published more than fifty books, became founder and organizer in 1887 of the Chicago Literary Schools. Brokmeyer was the medium through which the others gained insight into Hegel and his philosophy. Their aim was to "rationalize every field of activity, using Hegelian philosophy as a principle of interpretation."[40] Harris and Snider were particularly articulate in their protest "against the anti-institutional attitude of New England Transcendentalism which prized an isolated individualism, often developing into sheer eccentricity."[41]

In the end, however, there developed a harmony between the St. Louisans and the New Englanders as shown especially in the cordial relations between Emerson and Harris and the interaction between the St. Louis Movement and the Concord School of Philosophy, presided over by Bronson Alcott.

CHAPTER 4

Transcendental Journals and the Transcendentalist Aesthetic

W HATEVER else the Transcendentalists were, they were persons of an intellectual, an artistic, a literary inclination. Inspired as they were with the vision of a new and nobler way of life for mankind, it was natural for them to want to share their vision with others, and to do so not only by the spoken but also by the written word. It is not surprising then, to find them arduously engaged in the preparation of lectures, of essays, of poems given over to the presentation of their new philosophy. Established publications were not, however, always eager to print their output, with the result that they created their own journals as a means of circulating their ideas.

That the literary achievements of the Transcendentalists were best displayed in *The Dial*, a quarterly "Magazine for Literature, Philosophy and Religion" first published on July 1, 1840, seems unquestionable. The idea of establishing a Transcendental journal had been for years in the minds of some members of the Transcendental Club; and at a meeting of the club in September of 1839, the idea came to a head. Theodore Parker thought that Emerson should be editor, with Margaret Fuller and Hedge as assistants. But Emerson, jealous of his freedom, declined, and Miss Fuller was finally elected editor, with George Ripley agreeing to undertake the business end of the affair.[1] Despite his refusal to accept the editorship, Emerson was a bulwark to Miss Fuller, for he recommended and secured contributors for her and collaborated with her extensively in the introductory remarks, "The Editors to the Reader." Among those whose work appeared liberally in the pages of *The Dial* were Emerson himself, with both poems and essays; Miss Fuller, with several critical papers, an article on Goethe, and "The Great Lawsuit," later expanded into her book *Woman in the Nineteenth Century;* Bronson Alcott, with his Orphic sayings, which, in Frothingham's words, were "an amazement to the uninitiated and an amusement to the profane";[2] George Ripley; James Freeman Clarke; Theodore Parker; William H. Channing; Thoreau; Eliot Cabot; John S. Dwight; C.P. Cranch; and William Ellery Channing, the poet. Frothingham's summary of the nature of its contents is accurate and concise:

social tendencies were noticed; books were received; the newest picture, the last concert, was passed upon; judicious estimates were made of reforms and reformers abroad as well as at home; the philosophical discussions were able and discriminating; the theological papers were learned, broad and fresh. The four volumes are exceedingly rich in poetry, and poetry such as seldom finds a place in popular magazines.[3]

Although *The Dial* survived for only four years—with Emerson replacing Margaret Fuller after the first two years—, made no money, and never had more than three hundred subscribers, as Perry Miller has remarked, it "looms constantly larger in our cultural history—if only as a gallant effort to conduct a free and critical and literate journal."[4] In its literary criticism it regarded the moral element as the highest element in literature. It emphasized content over form and applauded the romantic ideas of inspiration, upwelling spirit, and conformity to internal truth. As Sidney Poger has said, "In its insistence on ideas, on sincerity, on life, and in its romantic judgments on the literature of its time, the criticism of *The Dial* helped bring about a flourishing of that literature, a flourishing which came to fruition in the American renaissance."[5]

Although the publication of *The Dial* coincided with the peak years of the Transcendental Movement, it was not the first journal to be dedicated to spreading the ideas and ideals of the movement. That distinction belongs to *The Western Messenger*, discussed briefly in the preceding chapter. Founded in Cincinnati in 1835, it lasted until 1841 and was influential in the East as well as in the Midwest, having "close to one hundred subscribers in New England alone."[6] In tone and content it was quite similar to *The Dial*, and it provided an early outlet for the publication of the poetry of Jones Very, one of the three best poets of the movement, the others being Emerson and Thoreau.[7]

"The powerful *Boston Quarterly Review*, the most philosophical of all the periodicals connected with the movement,"[8] was founded and edited by Orestes Brownson in 1838. Running the journal very nearly as a one-man job, Brownson, through the energy of his personality and the vividness of his prose style, made it play a major role in spreading Transcendental ideas throughout the country. When the *Christian Examiner*, the organ of literate Unitarianism, closed its doors to the Transcendentalists, Brownson's publication most effectively filled the gap. Like *The Dial*'s, its life was limited to four years, at the end of which time Brownson's enthusiasm for Transcendentalism was diminishing as he began to veer toward Roman Catholicism, to which he was finally converted.

William Henry Channing, nephew of the famous Dr. Channing, began in New York in 1843 a short-lived monthly called *The Present* to bring his ideas on reform before the public. Especially devoted to Fourierism, Channing and his writers were firm believers in perfectionism, and, although only seven issues were published before the magazine's demise in 1844, it managed to display many aspects of the general philosophy of the times.

The year 1843 also saw the birth of *The Phalanx*, edited by Albert Brisbane to spread the doctrines of Fourierism and the principles of Association. By 1845 it gave way to the more successful *Harbinger*, published as a weekly newspaper by the Brook Farm Phalanx until it moved to New York in 1847, following the closing of the Farm. Edited during its Brook Farm phase by George Ripley as a Fourierist organ, it became under Parke Godwin in New York a more general newspaper. It failed in 1849.

One of the more impressive of the progressive journals was *The Massachusetts Quarterly Review*, begun in 1847 and published until 1850. After Emerson and others had declined the editorship, Theodore Parker undertook it and promptly gave it the stamp of his forceful yet scholarly character. Chiefly interested in science, history, and philosophy—especially German romantic—it included pieces by Emerson and Thoreau as well as the best of Parker. Quite naturally, in view of Parker's strong feelings on the subject, it also espoused the cause of abolition.

Having vainly attempted in *The Present* to propagandize in behalf of "Christian Socialism," W. H. Channing made a second unsuccessful try in 1849 with his *Spirit of the Age*, published in New York until 1850.

One of the most promising of the new journals failed after publishing only a single issue. It was *Aesthetic Papers*, begun in 1849 with Elizabeth Peabody, whose Boston bookshop was a Transcendentalist haven, as editor. Ironically, one of the most widely reprinted essays ever written, Henry Thoreau's "Resistance to Civil Government," later retitled "On the Duty of Civil Disobedience," was included in its contents, as were "Main Street" by Hawthorne and "War" by Emerson. Gohdes speculates that the journal failed because the contents were so largely Transcendentalist. Whatever the cause, it promised to be what its editor desired, a worthy successor to *The Dial*, which she had published in its final two years. That Gohdes's speculation may be correct is supported by an interesting letter of August 29, 1842, from Carlyle to Emerson in response to the latter's invitation to write for *The Dial*.

I love your Dial, and yet it is with a kind of shudder. You seem to me in danger of dividing yourselves from the fact of this present universe, in which alone ugly as it is can I find any anchorage, and soaring away after Ideas, Beliefs, Revelations and such like,—into perilous altitudes as I think; beyond the curve of perpetual frost, for one thing! . . . Alas, it is so easy to screw oneself up into high and ever higher altitudes of Transcendentalism, and see nothing under one but the everlasting snows of Himmalayah, the Earth shrinking to a Planet, and the indigo firmament sowing itself with daylight stars; easy for you, for me: but whither does it lead? I dread always, to inanity, and more injuring of the lungs![9]

One of the more enduring aspects of such journals as *The Dial*, *The Western Messenger*, and *Aesthetic Papers* was the expression of Transcendentalist aesthetic theory that appeared in them. It must be recognized, of course, that, as Perry Miller has pointed out, "no two Transcendentalists could wholly agree upon any theoretical statement, particularly upon any theory of literature."[10] Nevertheless a similar attitude permeates the various statements and makes possible the construction of a generally held theme, marked only by variations.

Elizabeth Peabody, in the prefatory essay in her journal, discussed the meaning of the word "aesthetic." Admitting the difficulty of definition, she proclaimed that those of the Transcendental inclination use it to designate "that phase in human progress which subordinates the individual to the general, that he may appear on a higher plane of individuality."[11] In other words, the artist can realize his potential only by immersing himself in the Universal Being, some facet of which he is then able to express. Art, indeed, is nothing if it is not the "expression of the infinite by means of the beautiful."[12]

Emerson gives concrete support to this idea in his essay "The Poet," in which the Poet is referred to as "the man of Beauty." The true poet is an interpreter of nature, a kind of Aeolian harp through whom the winds of nature blow. Poetry, indeed, "was all written before time was," he says. Thus the best poet is he who is most delicately attuned to nature. Like Peabody Emerson holds that substance matters more than form: "For it is not metres, but a metre-making argument that makes a poem. . . ."[13]

John S. Dwight, in his theoretical explanation of music written for Miss Peabody's *Aesthetic Papers*, provides an extremely lucid statement of the Transcendental approach to art in general. By this word "beauty," he held, "is implied a soul, a moral end, a meaning of some sort, a something which makes it of interest to the inner life of man, which relates it to our invisible and real self. This beauty, like all other, results from the marriage of a spiritual fact with a material form, from the rendering external, and an object of sense, what lives in essence only in the soul."[14] Thus Dwight sees every genuine strain of music as "a serene prayer, or bold, inspired demand, to be united with all, at the Heart of things."[15] The work of art, then, grows out of the artist's need to plunge the self into the over-soul, the universal being, the ineffable One.

Alcott's view that "all creative minds have been inspired and guided by the law of unity"[16] echoes the same idea. And Margaret Fuller in the first number of *The Dial* (July, 1840) insisted on the unity that pervades true art. For her, nature is "the literature and art of the divine mind" and "human literature and art the criticism on that." Thus, as Marjorie Elder has observed, she agrees with Emerson's view of the all-pervading truth manifested as poetry in the midst of life's prose, and the view of the divinely inspired artist copying nature in a work of beauty structured to speak on both ideal and actual levels.[17]

Henry Thoreau, too, partakes of the Transcendental aesthetic in his insistence in *A Week on the Concord and Merrimack Rivers* on the fusion of art and life: "Art is not tame, and Nature is not

wild, in the ordinary sense. A perfect work of man's art would
also be wild or natural in a good sense."[18] And to be wild or
natural in a good sense means to be true to what actually is. The
aesthetic, then, insists that great art reflects reality. And, as in
Emerson's view, the ideal may also be reality. If we equate nature, which is real, with the Ideal, it then follows that a civilization that corrupts nature is unreal (note T.S. Eliot's insistence on
the unreality of the city in *The Wasteland*), and an art that reflects it only is also unreal. In the words of Norman Foerster,
"Art is therefore not idle play, nor a pleasurable expressive activity, but an arrestment and fixation of reality."[19]

Marjorie Elder's summing up of Emerson's aesthetic theory is
also a good summing up of the Transcendental aesthetic theory.
She suggests that it comprises three areas:

(his) view of Truth, his idea of the nature of the Artist, and his concept
of the Work of Art. His view of Truth will be discovered in his assertion
of the Real (the Perfect) shadowed in the Actual (the Imperfect)—in Nature and Man. His Artist will be seen as Representative Man, enabled
by faith, intuition, the pursuit of Beauty, and Nature's dynamic language, to become the Seer and Sayer. The Work of Art is an Expression
of Unity (Truth, Beauty) by variety (the symbol) made possible by the
action of Imagination on the Actual.[20]

A recent study of Emerson on poets and poetry, John Q.
Anderson's *The Liberating Gods*, further makes the point that
Emerson made the poet's intuition the test of truth and thereby
freed him "from the dominance of literary convention and the
past."[21] Emerson's attitude in this respect is clearly reflected in
virtually all of the criticism of literature and the other arts to appear in the various Transcendentalist publications.

CHAPTER 5

Emerson

IN a letter to his wife Lidian, written from Staten Island on
March 1, 1842, at the height of the Transcendental Movement,
Emerson speaks of dining with Horace Greeley and Albert Brisbane and complains of their fastening him in their thought to
Transcendentalism, "Whereof you know I am wholly guiltless,
and which is spoken of as a known and fixed element like salt or
meal: So that I have to begin by endless disclaimers and
explanations—'I am not the man you take me for.' "[1]

By that time quite generally acknowledged as the leading
spokesman of the movement, he still exhibited a resistance to
being labeled or to being associated in the public mind with any
group or movement. Indeed he went to some pains in his lecture
"The Transcendentalist" (delivered at the Masonic Temple in
Boston as the fourth in a series of eight lectures on "The Times"
in the winter of 1841–42 and printed in *The Dial* for January,
1843) to declare that "there is no such thing as a Transcendental
party, that there is no pure Transcendentalist. . . ."[2] He went on
to point out that the conversation and the poetry of the time
were deeply colored by the tendency to respect the intuitions
and to give them authority over experience. In his view Transcendentalism is an idealistic reaction against tradition and conven-
tionalism in every walk of life. Sherman Paul, indeed, contends
that Emerson's entire life was a rejection of the past.[3]

That Emerson had had Transcendental leanings at least as early
as 1822, when he was only nineteen, may be discerned from the
journal entry of June 16 of that year: "The evidence of things not
seen, is capable, I presume, of being made out as satisfactorily as
any thing subject to the eye of reason. . . ." He finds it necessary, in fact, "to feel after the evidence of *things not seen,* to explain the mazes of mortal things."[4] Only thus, we may infer, can

man attain to truth or to a knowledge of reality. Paul, as well as other Emerson scholars such as Paul Elmer More and Stephen Whicher, finds Emerson in the tradition of Jonathan Edwards a century earlier asking men to realize ideas with a sense of the heart as well as to entertain them intellectually.[5] Paul also sees Emerson's statement in the opening pages of *The Dial* as the most generally acceptable summing up of the Transcendentalists' demands.[6] "We do not wish," it reads, "to say pretty or curious things, or to reiterate a few propositions in varied forms, but, if we can, to give expression to that spirit which lifts men to a higher platform, restores to them the religious sentiment, brings them worthy aims and pure pleasures, purges the inward eye, makes life less desultory, and . . . reconciles the practical with the speculative powers."[7] The spirit so referred to may be summed up as a love of truth and of its work.

We may recall that, in the very month of September, 1836, when the Transcendental Club first met, Emerson had published his first book, *Nature*, in which, in a hundred pages, as Odell Shepard has remarked, he said "nearly every important thing that [he] or any other American transcendentalist would ever say. . . ."[8] It will be worthwhile, then, in the next few pages, to take a sharp look at this seminal volume.

Journal entries, letters, lectures and sermons predating publication show clearly that Emerson had been meditating on the subject matter of the book for at least ten years before its appearance. Only five hundred copies were printed, and the author's name did not even appear on the title page although Emerson seems to have made no other attempt to obscure its source. Within a month the five hundred copies were exhausted, but it was 1847 before the book was reissued. What reviews it received were either quite enthusiastic or extremely antagonistic.

Kenneth Burke has analyzed the structure of *Nature* thus: ". . .the everyday world . . . is to be interpreted as a *diversity* of *means* for carrying out a *unitary purpose* . . . that is situated in an ultimate realm *beyond* the here and now. The world's variety of things is thus to be interpreted *in terms of* a transcendent unifier (that infuses them all with its single spirit). And by this mode of interpretation all the world becomes viewed as a set of instrumentalities. . . . Emerson's brand of transcendentalism was but a short step ahead of out-and-out pragmatism."[9]

In the opening chapter, Emerson maintains that to love nature one must retain "the spirit of infancy even into the era of manhood."[10] For to love nature is to experience the delight and wonder of the child, as Wordsworth had suggested. The woods are pictured as having a rejuvenating influence, so much so that in the woods a man is always a child. Indeed it is there that Emerson suggests that he can lose his egotistical self and become one with God: "I become a transparent eyeball; I am nothing; I see all; the currents of the Universal Being circulate through me; I am part or parcel of God."[11] In this chapter, then, nature becomes the catalyst through which man achieves union with God. Thus the vital importance to man of enjoying a firsthand contact with nature.

Chapter 2 sketches the practical rather than the spiritual advantages that man owes to nature, "the prodigal provision that has been made for his support and delight on this green ball which floats him through the heavens."[12] The chapter ends on an interestingly Puritanical note: "A man is fed, not that he may be fed, but that he may work."[13] One gathers that we are here for a purpose, and that the purpose is that we may produce. No leaning, loafing, and inviting the soul as the more relaxed Whitman would have it.

Chapter 3 considers the nobler want of man that nature serves, the love of beauty. The aspects of beauty Emerson views as three: the delight in perceiving natural forms such as sky, mountains, animals, trees; the spiritual element, to be found in man's virtuous actions; and the intellectual element that finds expression in a work of art. Of these, the first two are fairly obvious. The third embodies the Emersonian aesthetic, or more broadly, the Transcendentalist aesthetic as noted in the preceding chapter. The mystery of humanity may be somewhat penetrated through a work of art, for such a work "is an abstract or epitome of the world. It is the result or expression of nature, in miniature."[14] Nature, then, works through man to produce beauty in the work of art, a minor image or symbol of itself.

Chapter 4 deals with language as dependent on nature for its force and power as an instrument to serve the needs of man. Good writing and brilliant discourse are seen as perpetual allegories: "This imagery is spontaneous. . . . It is proper creation."[15] Further, men who employ picturesque language are shown thereby to be in alliance with truth and God. Such language depends on the power to connect one's thought with its proper symbol.

Chapter 5 envisions nature as a discipline, for it exerts a moral influence on every individual. The degree of this influence is inestimable, but Emerson finds at its core the unity of nature, a unity in variety: "A leaf, a drop, a crystal, a moment of time, is related to the whole, and partakes of the perfection of the whole. Each particle is a microcosm, and faithfully renders the likeness of the world."[16] Such unity has its source in the universal spirit and also pervades thought and action, which are seen as human attributes and therefore superior to all others and preferred by the universal spirit.

Whicher sees these first five chapters as "designed to establish the dominion of Platonic Ideas over nature." Having established the primacy of ideas, Emerson breaks loose, he says, to accomplish his real revolution: "Outside is subjected to inside; the huge world comes round to the man." In the remainder of the book, man will be "finally cut adrift from the belief in any reality external to himself."[17]

Chapter 6, entitled "Idealism," holds that the advantage of the ideal theory over the popular faith is "that it presents the world in precisely that view which is most desirable to the mind. . . . Idealism sees the world in God. It beholds the whole circle of persons and things, of actions and events, of country and religion, not as painfully accumulated, atom after atom, act after act, in an aged creeping Past, but as one vast picture which God paints on the instant eternity for the contemplation of the soul."[18] This emphasis upon the present moment, upon the Everlasting Now, is a recurring theme among the Transcendentalists and is particularly marked in Emerson's thought. He describes himself, at one point, as "an endless seeker with no Past at my back." Thus the authority of institutions may be readily rejected as reflecting the dead hand of the past. The Idealist praises the God that is, not the God that was; he lives in the present, which is all there is.

Chapter 7, entitled "Spirit," describes nature as "the organ through which the universal spirit speaks to the individual, and strives to lead back the individual to it."[19] Spirit is the supreme being, which creates and is present throughout nature. In the degenerate state, man feels himself a stranger in nature and therefore alien to God. To know God, man must first feel at one with nature.

In Chapter 8, "Prospects," Emerson's essay rises to a grand, poetical finale. "Empirical science," he says, "is apt to cloud the sight, and by the very knowledge of functions and processes to bereave the student of the manly contemplation of the whole."[20] Only through intuitive wisdom is man able to achieve the sense of unity that lies at the core of the universe and to become what he was created to be, lord of the world "because he is its head and heart, and finds something of himself in every great and small thing, in every mountain stratum, in every new law of color, fact of astronomy, or atmospheric influence which observation or analysis lays open."[21] Quoting Plato's view that "poetry comes nearer to vital truth than history," Emerson ends his book by citing some lines that a certain Orphic poet[22] sang to him: " 'Nature is not fixed but fluid. Spirit alters, moulds, makes it. . . . Every spirit builds itself a house, and beyond its house a world, and beyond its world a heaven. Know then that the world exists for you. For you is the phenomenon perfect. What we are, that only can we see. All that Adam had, all that Caesar could, you have and can do. . . . Build therefore your own world. As fast as you conform your life to the pure idea in your mind, that will unfold its great proportions.' " With the influx of spirit, " 'the Kingdom of man over nature, which cometh not with observation—a dominion such as now is beyond his dream of God—he shall enter without more wonder than the blind man feels who is gradually restored to sight.' "[23]

Cameron sees the whole argument of *Nature* summed up in these Orphic lines, the ten years (1825–1835) of Emerson's philosophic development symbolized in them, and regards them as the "first trumpet blast of New England Transcendentalism."[24] Surely the idea that man must find his salvation not through the mediation of other men, even the best, but through achieving a sense of union with the universal being by means of establishing a primary contact with nature and asserting his primacy over it was one that fired the imaginations of most of those who were to become known as Transcendentalists.

The publication of *Nature* marked the beginning of Emerson's great creative decade, a decade that coincides with the flood tide of the Transcendental Movement. Largely on the strength of the reputation he had achieved through his first book, he was invited in 1837 to deliver the Phi Beta Kappa address at Harvard College. Entitled "The American Scholar," it reiterated the message of *Nature*. To know yourself, study nature. Be Man thinking, not a bookworm, tyrannized over by the recorded thoughts of others. Translate thought into action, for only so much do you know as you have lived. Trust yourself and never defer to the popular cry. Be free and brave. Remember that "the world is nothing, the man is all; in yourself is the law of all nature, and you know not yet how a globule of sap ascends; in yourself slumbers the whole of Reason [Spirit or Soul]; it is for you to know all; it is for you to dare all."[25] Finally, Emerson admonishes the young American scholars to turn their backs on "the courtly muses of Europe" and look to their own time and place for their inspiration. The entire address vibrates with a sense of optimism and confidence in the ability of the young men and the young nation to achieve greatness rivaling that of ancient Greece and Rome.

Some six years before, Emerson had resigned as pastor to the Second Church at Boston, having become disenchanted with the ministry and with the formalism of churches generally. But he had maintained his connections with many of his Unitarian friends and, after the striking success of the Phi Beta Kappa address, it did not come as a total surprise that representatives of the senior class of the Harvard Divinity School should have written to invite him to deliver the commencement talk. He accepted with alacrity because he would now have an ideal platform from which to present his radical views on the current theocracy. The "Divinity School Address" of July 15, 1838, proved to be an intellectual grenade exploded in the very halls of authority. The man who is just at heart is God. One mind is active everywhere, and whatever opposes it is defeated. Good is positive, evil negative. The perception of the law that benevolence is absolute and real, whereas evil is death or nonentity, awakens in us the religious sentiment, which lies at the foundation of society. But primary faith is intuitive and cannot be gained through the mediation of another. Thus "historical Christianity has fallen into the error that corrupts all attempts to communicate religion."[26] It has made of Jesus a demigod by dwelling on his person and inviting men to subordinate their natures to Christ's nature, accepting its interpretations of that nature. The church has become virtually defunct through its formalism and has destroyed the power of preaching "by withdrawing it from the exploration of the moral nature of man."[27]

Finally, Emerson warns the fledgling ministers to be themselves, cast aside conformity, and "acquaint men at first hand with Deity."[28] Thus will the church be reformed, through soul, soul, and more soul.

This rejection of orthodox religion and its collateral attack on the organized church brought forth cries of outrage from the elders of the Divinity School and their followers in the ministry and shouts of delight from the Transcendentalist camp. It would be almost three decades before Emerson would again be invited to speak at Harvard.

Whicher views the address as "a most revealing example of Emerson's highly Puritanical rebellion against Puritanism."[29] He finds Emerson deserting the Unitarian God in order to worship moral perfection, which had two aspects, one coming from the moralistic discipline of Unitarianism, the other from the tradition of Calvinistic piety—the sense of duty and the sentiment of virtue reminiscent of Jonathan Edwards. Nature is substituted for revelation as the ground for faith, and moral law and moral sentiment are the reality of nature.[30]

From the standpoint of their contribution to Transcendentalism, the most important of the *Essays* that appeared in 1841 are the famous "Self-Reliance" and "The Over-Soul." As Rusk shows, the first of these had been, of all the essays, longest in his mind.[31] As early as February 10, 1833, he had been recording in his journal such thoughts as "Myself is much more than I know, and yet I know nothing else."[32] The essay fairly radiates assurance and belief in the capacity of Everyman for genius. If we fail to achieve our grand potential, it is only because we have failed to trust ourselves. Rid yourself of the twin terrors of consistency and conformity, and you will be a man. Society, being in conspiracy against the manhood of its members, is averse to self-reliance. Central, then, to achieving the self-trust that alone can free man from his bondage to society is the tenet: "No law can be sacred to me but that of my nature. . . . the only right is what is after my constitution; the only wrong what is against it."[33]

Reiterating the theme of the "Divinity School Address," he asserted that "the relations of the soul to the divine spirit are so

pure that it is profane to seek to interpose helps."[34] Nor would
he accept the conventional view of prayer. "Prayer," he confidently asserted, "is the contemplation of the facts of life from the
highest point of view. It is the soliloquy of a beholding and jubil-
ant soul. . . . As soon as the man is at one with God, he will not
beg."[35] Prayer, then, is a celebration of the works of God, not a
means of effecting a private end.

The final shot in his fusillade was reserved for society's reliance
on property, including the reliance on governments which protect
it: "Men have looked away from themselves and at things so long
that they have come to esteem the religious, learned and civil institutions as guards of property, and they deprecate assaults on
these, because they feel them to be assaults on property. They
measure their esteem of each other by what each has, and not by
what each is."[36]

Perhaps no single work of Emerson called forth more strenuous
reaction, pro and con. The Transcendentalists generally applauded it; but others, some of them among his closest suppor-
ters, like his Aunt Mary Moody Emerson, rejected it out of hand.
A "strange medley of atheism and false independence" she
branded it while questioning the sanity of its author.[37] Even such
an astute modern critic as Stephen Whicher sees the Emerson of
"Self-Reliance" as a vain dreamer trying to confront the pressures
of his world by creating "a heroic personality endowed with a
supreme power before which they would vanish."[38]

What many of Emerson's critics have missed in their reading of
"Self-Reliance" is the true nature of his admonition to "Trust thy-
self." The self referred to is nothing but the divine spirit of which
man is part and parcel. Thus, by trusting the self, man is but confiding himself to the all-embracing, benevolent universal being or
over-soul that is the center and unifying agent of all things. By so
trusting, man cannot but go aright. Viewed thus, the seeming arrogance, the apparent glorification of any kind of individualism
vanish in the most basic of Transcendental concepts.

This concept received its most detailed treatment in the essay
"The Over-Soul." In a key passage Emerson speaks of

that Unity, that Over-Soul, within which every man's particular being is
contained and made one with all other; that common heart of which all
sincere conversation is the worship, to which all right action is submis-

sion; that overpowering reality which confutes our tricks and talents, and constrains every one to pass for what he is, and to speak from his character and not from his tongue, and which evermore tends to pass into our thought and hand and become wisdom and virtue and power and beauty. We live in succession, in division, in parts, in particles. Meantime within man is the soul of the whole; the wise silence; the universal beauty, to which every part and particle is equally related; the eternal ONE. And this deep power in which we exist and whose beatitude is all accessible to us, is not only self-sufficing and perfect in every hour, but the act of seeing and the thing seen, the seer and the spectacle, the subject and the object, are one.[39]

Of all the subjects Emerson's mind grappled with, the subject of soul has received the most attention in modern scholarship. Jonathan Bishop, who has devoted an entire book to it, defines it as the sense of being. In consequence, he contends, Emerson speaks of it as single, the same for all men.[40] It consists "of a conjunction of the organic faculty, the intellect, and the moral sentiment. . . ."[41] Delving into the influences that helped to shape Emerson's approach, Harrison sees them as primarily Platonic or, more particularly, Neoplatonic. The Neoplatonists' interpretation of Plato was, he holds, vital to Emerson, in that "they consider the highest idea in Plato's scheme of metaphysics the idea of the One as it is treated in the *Parmenides*."[42] Harrison, however, sees Emerson as using them to create his own conception of soul. Thus he finds it in all creation, although his main purpose is to assert its presence, the divine presence, in man, who experiences it in a mystical resolution of his own life into that of the divine.[43]

Cameron and Whicher, however, see Coleridge as preeminent in shaping Emerson's view of the soul. Cameron devotes much space in his *Emerson the Essayist* to this contention, showing that from 1825 to 1836 Emerson had Coleridge's works always on his desk and that the early *Journals* reveal Coleridge's ideas more than those of any other author. And Whicher believes Emerson's discovery of Coleridge to be the turning point that led him to think that the soul of man *is* God. Indeed this idea, that God is *within* man, Whicher sees as so revolutionary that it was the real reason for Emerson's resigning his ministry.[44]

The most significant journal entry prior to the writing of the over-soul essay to show that, whatever his sources, Emerson had thoroughly absorbed and made his own his thinking on the soul is that of May 26, 1837, which reads:

Who shall define to me an Individual? I behold with awe & delight many illustrations of the One Universal Mind. I see my being imbedded in it. As a plant in the Earth so I grow in God. I am only a form of him. He is the soul of Me. I can even with a mountainous aspiring say, *I am God*, by transferring my *Me* out of the flimsy & unclean precincts of my body, my fortunes, my private will, & meekly retiring upon the holy austerities of the Just & the Loving—upon the secret fountains of Nature.[45]

The term "over-soul" Carpenter believes to be original with Emerson. As he points out, the Neoplatonists had used the terms "world soul" and "universal soul."[46] James E. Miller, Jr. has made the interesting suggestion that it is possible to view Emerson's terms "soul" and "over-soul" as modern psychology's "conscious" and "unconscious," or the personal as differentiated from the collective unconscious.[47] In the final analysis, however, it is impossible not to agree with Rusk's conclusion that "Emerson, the theorizer of mysticism, found the actual revelations of the Over-Soul as incommunicable and indescribable as the practicing mystic usually found his experiences to be."[48]

It is interesting to note that, although Emerson has been considered by many important critics from his own time to ours as, in Paul Elmer More's words, the outstanding figure of American letters,[49] he has been found wanting in a variety of ways by many others. At the height of the Transcendental Movement, Christopher P. Cranch, after attending Emerson's lecture course on the Age, wrote to Miss Julia Myers on February 4, 1840:

Emerson is to me the master mind of New England, at least so far as depth and wonderful beauty in thought, rare and eloquent delivery go. . . . Emerson's doctrines, however, are considered very heretical by most persons, and by as many, downright atheism, mysticism, or perhaps nonsense. Horace Mann being asked the other day by a lady how he liked Mr. Emerson, "Madam," said he, "a Scotch mist is perfect sunshine to him!"[50]

Such leaders of the Boston intellectual establishment as Edward Everett, John Quincy Adams, and Andrews Norton had little but scorn for him. Adams and Norton thought him an atheist and a heretic. Everett spoke of his "conceited, laborious nonsense." The Cambridge theologians termed him a pantheist and a German mystic with the style founded on Neoplatonic moonshine.[51] Even such sensitive artists as Hawthorne and Melville, touched as they themselves were by the Transcendental mode, were severe in their judgments. Hawthorne in a journal entry of August 15, 1842, refers to ". . .Mr. Emerson—the mystic, stretching his hand out of cloud-land, in vain search for something real. . . . Mr. Emerson is a great searcher for facts; but they seem to melt away and become insubstantial in his grasp."[52] Melville, in a letter to Evert Duyckinck, mentions being agreeably surprised at an Emerson lecture and says, "I love all men who *dive*," but he tempers this compliment with the remark, "I could readily see in Emerson, notwithstanding his merit, a gaping flaw. It was, the insinuation, that had he lived in those days when the world was made, he might have offered some valuable suggestions."[53] Marjorie Elder has competently summed up his objections to Emersonian Transcendentalism as "centered in three faults that he found in the philosophy: it tended to pride, it lacked 'heart,' and it was too idealistic, lacking physical zest."[54] And surely the fuzzy-headed philosopher, Plotinus Plinlimmon, of Melville's bitter novel *Pierre*, is a caricature of Emerson.

At the beginning of our own century, George Santayana rephrased many of these same objections in his essay "Emerson." "At bottom," he wrote, "he had no doctrine at all. The deeper he went and the more he tried to grapple with fundamental conceptions, the vaguer and more elusive they became in his hands. Did he know what he meant by Spirit or the 'Over-Soul'? Could he say what he understood by the terms, so constantly on his lips, Nature, Law, God, Benefit, or Beauty? He could not. . . ."[55] The one supreme gift that Santayana acknowledges in Emerson is that of poetic imagination, for which he could be forgiven a great deal.

Floyd Stovall has outlined what he conceives to be the current charges against Emerson:

1. A transcendental impracticability in worldly matters.
2. A blindness to sin and evil.
3. A hostility to reform of social and political evils.
4. A belief in perfectibility in this world.
5. A worship of self-reliant spontaneity over the authority of tradition.

6. A beneficent and sentimental religious belief that equates individualistic impulse with the voice of God.[56]

Let us attempt to weigh these charges without advocacy: That Emerson was not a man of the world in a business or counting-house sense seems perfectly true. He would lecture for nothing if he were told that those who wanted to hear him could not afford a fee. His business was not the making of money but the making of minds. The charge, then, may be sustained, but, from one point of view, it is more a compliment than a condemnation.

In his autobiography the great Irish poet William Butler Yeats remarks that Emerson, along with Whitman, begins to seem superficial because he lacks the Vision of Evil. It is a view that Hawthorne and Melville in Emerson's own time as well as countless critics in ours have embraced. But how true is it to the evidence?

In his admirably thorough biography Rusk finds Emerson at the age of nineteen "finding the problem of evil tough. He thought no elaborate argument could remove the stubborn fact of the Existence of Evil, and Evil was the foremost difficulty in the way of belief in an omnipotent good Principle. . . . There was indeed 'a huge and disproportionate abundance of evil on Earth,' and the good was 'but a little island of light amidst the unbounded ocean.' "[57] By the time he came to the writing of the "Divinity School Address," he thought he had found that omnipotent good principle, apparently in the Neoplatonic doctrine so forcefully expressed by Plotinus that real existence or being is by definition good; therefore, if evil exists, it can only be in the sphere of nonbeing. Thus Emerson wrote: "Good is positive. Evil is merely privative, not absolute: it is like cold, which is the privation of heat."[58] Or later, in "Compensation," he writes, "Being is the vast affirmative, excluding negation, self-balanced, and swallowing up all relations, parts and times within itself. Nature, truth, virtue, are the influx from thence. Vice is the absence or departure of the same. Nothing, Falsehood, may indeed stand as the great Night or shade on which as a background the living universe paints itself forth, but no fact is begotten by it; it cannot work, for it is not."[59]

As Newton Arvin has pointed out, Augustine in *The City of God* arrived through his Neoplatonic reading at a very similar position: "Evil has no positive nature, but the loss of good has received the name 'evil.' "[60] What Arvin correctly contends is that the viewpoint Emerson had come to by 1838 was not original with him but "had a long and august tradition behind it in Western thought and analogies with the thought not only of Europe but of the East."[61]

By midcentury, when Emerson wrote "Fate," he clearly showed that he was quite as conscious as Melville of the unrelenting savagery of nature. The citing of earthquakes, volcanic eruptions, famine and plague, predatory animal behavior is an admission of "the odious facts" of life. Man is the prisoner of circumstance and of his heredity. And, as Arvin has also observed, Emerson in his 1844 address at Concord, "Emancipation in the British West Indies," was acutely aware of the existence of evil in the relations of human beings. The wealthy planters he saw as "full of vices; their children were lumps of pride, sloth, sensuality and rottenness. The position of woman was nearly as bad as it could be; and, like other robbers, they could not sleep in security."[62]

In balance, then, whereas it is true that the prevailing wind in Emerson's thinking is optimistic and the vision of Evil therefore is not central, it is untrue to believe of him that he was blind to the existence of sin and evil in the scheme of things.

As to his being hostile to the reform of social and political evils, it is true that he recoiled from active participation in reform movements, many of which he lists in the lecture "New England Reformers" of 1844. To become intensely involved in any one would be to run the risk of not being able to see the forest for the trees. Further, such movements might be destructive of individual force. Reform of society must begin with reform of the individual through his own effort. We remember that his objection to Brook Farm was that it would imprison him more than he was; and the same was true of all cooperative reform schemes. Nonetheless Whicher sees him as generally sympathetic to the idea of reform and advances the concept that his idea of the scholar taking an active role in life and providing for his own needs through a primary relation with nature was the precursor to Thoreau's Walden experiment and to Brook Farm as well.[63] One may also cite his support of the abolition of slavery—belated though some found it—and his defense of equal rights for women in respect to property and voting. As to reforming political evils, his attitude may be best summed up in his confession that the motto of the Boston *Globe* is so attractive to him that he has small appetite for reading much of what is below it in its columns. The motto read: "The world is governed too much."[64] Perhaps the journal entry for September 3, 1833, sums up best his basic position. It reads: "A man contains all that is needful to his government within himself. He is made a law unto himself. All real good or evil that can befall him must be from himself. He only can do himself any good or any harm. Nothing can be given to him or taken from him but always there is a compensation. There is a correspondence between the human soul & everything that exists in the world."[65]

That Emerson had implicit faith in the ability of man to improve if not to perfect himself in this world is certainly true. He was quite capable of discerning, as in the essay entitled "Napoleon; Man of the World," "the universal imbecility, indecision and indolence of men,"[66] but his dominant belief is in man's power to achieve his potential, which is godlike. And how can this happy state be brought about? The answer appears to lie in proper education, at the root of which is inspiration. A journal entry of April 20, 1834, speaks to the point: "the whole secret of the teacher's force lies in the conviction that men are convertible. And they are. They want awakening."[67]

Any student of Emerson must, of course, agree that he was on the side of self-reliant spontaneity as against the authority of tradition. In being so, he was at one with the advanced thought of his time, certainly with what may be called Transcendental thought. As Goddard has remarked, the battle cries of Transcendentalism, born in France, were Away with tradition! Back to Nature! Down with creeds and institutions! The Golden Age is before us![68] And as Howard Mumford Jones has cogently observed, the European revolutionary movements of 1830 and 1848 reinforced an individualistic philosophy of life in America—as did social philosophies like Fourierism, theological systems like Lutheranism, and politico-economic ideologies like Benthamism.[69]

The question whether Emerson's attitude is wise or foolish can be answered by the individual only on the basis of his own philosophic bent. If he believes in the inherent freedom of the individual and the fundamental goodness (or *god*ness) of man, he will see Emerson as "the wisest American." If, on the other hand, he regards man as inherently weak, wicked, and needful of the constant discipline of authority, he will find Emerson little more than a foolish, romantic dreamer or peddler of mist and moonshine.

That Emerson embraced "a beneficent and sentimental religion that equates individualistic impulse with the voice of God" is a charge that suffers from the same defects as that of a biased judge to an innocent jury: namely, the use of connotative language with derogatory overtones to garb a statement that is at best a half-truth. If Emerson is being charged with believing in the power of good to triumph over the power of evil, if he is being charged with believing in the primacy of the heart over the head or intuition over calculation, the charge is correct. To say, however, that such belief equates mere individualistic impulse with the voice of God is to distort the belief. What Emerson is saying is that, if God is to be found, man must look within the self; that man is divine through union with the over-soul that contains all; that man enters into such union through a mystic experience to be had only through a primary contact with nature.

One further charge not to be found on Stovall's list has been leveled at Emerson, namely, that he was not sufficiently original but took his main ideas from others. This, of course, raises the basic issue of whether or not thought or art can ever be original in the sense of being something entirely new under the sun. When he remarks in "The American Scholar" that each age must write its own books, he does not mean that it must put aside the experience of the past but rather express it anew in its own terms. "What you have aggregated in a natural manner," he says in "Intellect," "surprises and delights when it is produced. For we cannot oversee each other's secret."[70] The philosopher or the artist must build on what has gone before, but he must come to it with his own eyes and take from it only what serves to inspire his own thought and feeling.

Of course Emerson was much influenced by other writers. We have already noted the hold of Platonic and Neoplatonic thought on him as well as his avid pursuit of Oriental scriptures. There was German romantic philosophy, too, that Emerson Marks sees as coming to him largely through Coleridge and Carlyle, although "Cousin taught him his Hegel and much of his Fichte."[71] Slater believes Carlyle's early essays in the *Edinburgh Review* provided him and the other Transcendentalists with "an introduction to the Kantian conception of space and time as mere categories of the understanding, and a loose and popular definition of *transcendental*—'ascending beyond the senses'—which was to be adequate for most of their needs."[72] But Nicoloff sees Carlyle's influence on Emersonian thought as much less than usually suggested, although he agrees that *Sartor Resartus* (1836) gave Emerson a powerful boost in his early radical idealism. Importantly, he sees the two men as using Kantian transcendentalism out of basically different motives: Carlyle to escape the machine world of eighteenth-century science and philosophy, Emerson to establish further the primacy of mind over matter.[73] We might multiply instances of literary or philosophic or religious influence on Emerson a hundred times over; but what should not be overlooked is that he used his materials as every great artist has always done—to create his own peculiar fabric, which bears his initials some way in the corner.

Emerson, in his turn, influenced a host of other thinkers and writers, some of them bearing names that are met with greater applause in contemporary critical circles than is his. As Bishop has convincingly observed, Thoreau, Whitman, William James, and Melville were all much influenced by Emerson even though their admission of the fact is grudging, except for Whitman, who reminds us that he was simmering and Emerson brought him to a boil.[74]

In closing this chapter, one should at least note the change that occurred in Emerson from the heyday of the Transcendental Movement to the time of his backward look in "Historic Notes of Life and Letters in New England"(1867). Those who have studied his thought most closely all remark it. Bishop suggests that Emerson the romantic becomes Emerson the Victorian by the 1850s.[75] Whicher sees him gradually undergoing a change in which, for all his trust in soul, he seeks a philosophy of experience:

If the keynote of his early thought is revolution, that of his later thought is acquiescence and optimism. From an intense rebellion against the world in the name of the Soul, he moved to a relative acceptance of things as they are, world and Soul together; from teaching men their power to rise above fate, he turned to teaching them how to make the best of it.[76]

And Paul sees the Emerson who wrote "Historic Notes" as taking an almost antiquarian interest in the age in which Transcendentalism blossomed as a revolt against formalism, the result of which was a return to a higher law "of self-affirming individual perception."[77]

What appears to have happened is that, as Emerson rubbed shoulders more and more with the world of men on his march to the grave, the flame of the old Transcendental idealism, the dream of man's perfectibility on Earth, grew dimmer and dimmer until it was all but extinguished in a skepticism that was virtually antitranscendental.

CHAPTER 6

Thoreau

IF Ralph Waldo Emerson was the chief expositor of Transcendentalism, Henry David Thoreau was surely its chief practitioner. His most authoritative biographer, Walter Harding, has remarked that there is scarcely a major principle of the Transcendental Movement that he did not espouse. "And in the long run," according to Harding, "he held more closely to its fundamental principles than did any of the others. He was a true Transcendentalist to the end of his life. Whether he was experimenting in life at Walden Pond, going to jail for refusing to pay his poll tax, or defending John Brown's action at Harpers Ferry, he was operating from a base of Transcendentalist principles."[1]

Exactly when Emerson and Thoreau came to know one another as friends is uncertain, but by the autumn of 1837 they were beginning to see much of each other. Fourteen years younger than Emerson, Thoreau was then a recent graduate of Harvard College and a resident of Concord, where he had been born and raised. Although Emerson wished to found no schools and to have no disciples, he found in Thoreau the living representation of his ideal American scholar, and Thoreau for his part found in the author of the newly published *Nature* a man whose ideas were both a challenge and a promise. The friendship blossomed, and although, like love, its course never did run smooth, it was to mean much to both men.

Remembering his young friend of many years before in his essay "Thoreau," written in 1884, Emerson says of him that he

was sincerity itself, and might fortify the convictions of prophets in the ethical laws by his holy living. . . . A truth-speaker he, capable of the most deep and strict conversation; a physician to the wounds of any soul; a friend, knowing not only the secret of friendship, but almost worshipped by those few persons who resorted to him as their confessor and prophet, and knew the deep value of his mind and great heart.[2]

But, although proclaiming that "No truer American existed than Thoreau,"[3] he must show the other side of the coin and profess a degree of disappointment with his friend: "Had his genius been only contemplative, he had been fitted to his life, but with his energy and practical ability he seemed born for great enterprise and for command; and I so much regret the loss of his rare powers of action, that I cannot help counting it a fault in him that he had no ambition."[4] Emerson was, however, not alone in this feeling; as Carl Bode has pointed out, when Thoreau died, he was "a disappointment to most people who knew him."[5] As with most men and women who have achieved a fame that endures, it remained for future generations to appreciate his true worth. Not that the more discerning of his contemporaries were blind to it. Hawthorne, for example, although finding him, "like other humorists . . . an intolerable bore,"[6] viewed him as "a healthy and wholesome man to know." In a journal entry for September 1, 1842, Hawthorne speaks of Thoreau's keen observation of nature, his closeness to the Indian way of life, his good writing, and his true taste for poetry, "although more exclusive than is desirable, like all other Transcendentalists. . . ."[7] The majority, however, saw Thoreau not only as a disciple but also as an imitator of his friend Emerson. It was a cloud that Thoreau had to live under from the time the relationship ripened to the end of his days.

Perhaps no one has better revealed the basic difference between Emerson and Thoreau than Joel Porte in his book *Emerson and Thoreau; Transcendentalists in Conflict.* Emerson, he suggests, is all intellect, whereas Thoreau is dominated by the senses. Together, he intimates, they make the complete Transcendentalist, for he sees both the intellectual and the sensuous as necessary to an adequate definition of Transcendentalism: "Because he was always convinced of the rightness and nobility of a life lived in conformity only to the highest dictates of the conscience, Emerson never ceased trying to instruct his readers in the dangers of fleshly subversion: 'Why should we be the dupes of our senses. . . ?' Thoreau, on the other hand, was certain that a wise man 'will confine the observations of his mind as closely as possible to the experience or life of his senses. . .' "[8] Emerson, Porte points out, stressed the moral law, the subordination of passions to the will, whereas Thoreau warned his friend Harrison Blake, "Do not be too moral. You may cheat yourself out of much life so."[9] Seeing Emerson's denial of the body as a conscious attempt to forestall the tragic loss of physical vitality, Porte thus believes the true theme of Emerson's essay "The Tragic" to be that he who would avoid danger must practice detachment. Thoreau, however, is seen as insisting that the only real joy is of the body; the sexual instinct, "the embodiment of the will to live," is at the heart of his writings.[10] It is, at least, suggestive that it was Emerson, the twice married man, not Thoreau, the perennial bachelor, who confided to his journal at the age of thirty-nine, "I have so little vital force that I could not stand the dissipation of a flowing and friendly life; I should die of consumption in three months. But now I husband all my strength in this bachelor life I lead; no doubt I shall be a well-preserved old gentleman."[11]

It must, nevertheless, be borne in mind that Thoreau did not denigrate or deny the importance of spirit. Indeed, he attempted to strike a balance between the physical and the spiritual. A key passage in the "Higher Laws" chapter of *Walden* reads: "I found in myself, and still find, an instinct toward a higher, or, as it is named, spiritual life, as do most men, and another toward a primitive rank and savage one, and I reverence them both. I love the wild not less than the good."[12] In the light of such a statement, it is not difficult to sustain Goddard's view of Thoreau as the true Yankee-mystic, maintaining a much better balance between the real and the ideal than did Emerson.[13]

There is no doubt that Thoreau speaks more effectively to our own time than does Emerson. His advocacy of anarchy, his theory of civil disobedience, his insistence on simplifying life, his delight in nature, his straightforward style of expression have all found a ready response among modern readers, who have become increasingly attracted to his books, particularly *Walden*, as the twentieth century has progressed.

Apparently at Emerson's suggestion Thoreau began in 1837 to keep a journal. As the years went by it became, even more than Emerson's own voluminous journal, a remarkable record throughout its thousands of pages of one man's observations on the world around him—its people, places, and objects—as well as his thoughts on the life of the spirit. As Carl Bode has so well said, "The journal is the record of a man who made what he observed part of himself and in the process made himself a great writer."[14] And, as with Emerson, Thoreau made the journal the initial repository of the ideas, experiences, and meditations that were later to find fuller or more polished expression in his published work.

Like Emerson, Thoreau tried lecturing, but unlike his mentor he was never truly successful in the medium. Lacking Emerson's sonorous voice and commanding presence, viewing his audiences with a degree of suspicion if not of hostility, and fearful of losing his integrity by trying to please them, he was never thoroughly at ease on the platform. As he complained to his journal the night of December 6, 1854, after the failure of "Getting a Living" (posthumously published as "Life Without Principle"), "I feel that I am in danger of cheapening myself by trying to become a successful lecturer, *i.e.*, to interest my audience. I fail to get even the attention of the mass. I should suit them better if I suited myself less."[15] Nonetheless the lectures were often a valuable proving ground for work that he intended to publish.

From the standpoint of Transcendentalism, the most important of Thoreau's published writings are *Walden* and two shorter pieces, "On the Duty of Civil Disobedience" and "Life Without Principle."

Published in 1854, *Walden* had its beginnings in Thoreau's famous experiment in living "deliberately," in fronting "only the essential facts of life," to "see if I could not learn what it had to teach and not, when I came to die, discover that I had not lived."[16] In March of 1845 Ellery Channing wrote to him from New York with the suggestion that he build a hut on Walden Pond and write the book he had long been contemplating about the trip he and his brother John had taken in 1839 on the Concord and Merrimack Rivers. It seems that he promptly adopted the suggestion, borrowed an axe from Bronson Alcott, and got permission from Emerson to fell some trees on a woodlot he owned by the pond and build himself a small cottage.[17] With fitting symbolism he moved into the newly completed ten by fifteen foot cabin on July 4, 1845. Now began his grand experiment in practicing the self-reliance Emerson had preached so ardently. For two years, two months, and two days he lived simply and ate plainly with no cost to himself save some six weeks' labor out of each year given over to planting and cultivating crops and doing odd jobs of carpentering and surveying. He proved to his own satisfaction that it is quite possible for a man to live quite sufficiently in New England with minimal physical effort provided he restricts his wants to the essentials of food, clothing, and shelter, and to have virtually unlimited time in which to indulge his interests in reading, writing, and observing the natural world around him.

Many of Thoreau's fellow Concordians were much interested in knowing why he, a Harvard graduate, had given up civilized life to go live in a woodland hut. In consequence he began writing a series of lectures to be given at the Concord Lyceum to answer their questions. These eventually grew into the book *Walden,* which, however, took seven years and eight complete revisions to finish to his satisfaction.[18]

Although the material set down in his journal covers in great detail the more than two years spent at Walden Pond, it became clear to the concerned author that his book needed a plan of organization. Therefore he finally adopted the idea of condensing the time into a single year and arranging the chronicle in order of the cycle of seasons: summer, fall, winter, spring. It was a brilliant stroke that greatly simplified his problem of creating order out of his diverse materials by providing a natural skeleton for the work.

Walden, like all profound books, can be read at many levels. Without doubt it, along with *Nature* and *Leaves of Grass,* is one of the three great Transcendentalist masterpieces. However one may read it, certain main ideas shine through:

1. That man, made to be free, has not only been enslaved but, more tragic still, has enslaved himself.
2. That the highroad to individual freedom is self-reliance gained through simplifying life.
3. That health and happiness can best be achieved through living in close contact with nature.
4. That truth is the ultimate desideratum, to be valued more than love, money, or fame.

In the long opening chapter entitled "Economy" Thoreau sees his neighbors as living lives of quiet desperation, chained to their farms, their cattle, their shops: "It is hard to have a Southern overseer; it is worse to have a Northern one; but worst of all when you are the slave-driver of yourself."[19] And to what end do his neighbors enslave themselves? To gain material goods and live a more "comfortable" life. And such an end keeps their noses to the grindstone and prevents any elevation of spirit. "Most of the luxuries, and many of the so-called comforts of life, are not only not indispensable, but positive hindrances to the elevation of mankind."[20] Thus also the stream of scientific inventions that so complicate a man's life as to further enslave rather than free him.

It follows, then, that if a man desires to be free he must first divest himself of the encumbrances of a life of luxury. To do so is to take the first step toward being a philosopher or wise man, says Thoreau. "To be a philosopher is not merely to have subtle thoughts, but so to love wisdom as to live according to its dictates, a life of simplicity, independence, magnanimity, and trust. It is to solve some of the problems of life, not only theoretically, but practically."[21] In a spiritual sense, then, a kind of voluntary poverty is the greatest riches. Time spent in securing, maintaining, and guarding material possessions is time lost from the primary business of enriching the inner self.

In the chapter "Where I Lived, And What I Lived For" Thoreau remarks that "the millions are awake enough for physical labor; but only one in a million is awake enough for effective intellectual exertion, only one in a hundred millions to a poetic or divine life. To be awake is to be alive."[22] He follows this assertion with the thoroughly Transcendental remark that "I know of no more encouraging fact than the unquestionable ability of man to elevate his life by a conscious endeavor. It is something to be able to paint a particular picture, or to carve a statue, and so to make a few objects beautiful; but it is far more glorious to carve and paint the very atmosphere and medium through which we look, which morally we can do. To affect the quality of the day, that is the highest of arts."[23] The means, then, to elevate one's life is to simplify it, to live as deliberately as nature, to observe steadily realities only and not allow oneself to be deluded by petty fears and petty pleasures.

Men, Thoreau says, think of truth as remote, "behind the farthest star, before Adam and after the last man."[24] What they fail to recognize is that truth is here and now: "God himself culminates in the present moment, and will never be more divine in the lapse of all the ages. And we are enabled to apprehend at all what is sublime and noble only by the perpetual instilling and drenching of the reality that surrounds us."[25]

Harding refers to *Walden* as "a guide book to the higher life,"[26] which it surely is, a Transcendental signpost that advises us to follow the unique spirit within us rather than the highways of the world, rutted deep in tradition and conformity. "I learned this, at least, by my experiment," Thoreau tells us, "that if one advances confidently in the direction of his dreams, and endeavors to live the life which he has imagined, he will meet with a success unexpected in common hours. . . . If you have built castles in the air, your work need not be lost; that is where they should be. Now put the foundations under them."[27]

Whereas *Walden* deals with the life close to nature, the means of achieving personal freedom, and the individual's progress toward truth by fixing his gaze on reality, Thoreau was by no means blind to the vexing social issues of his time. Morally incensed by the Mexican War and the passage of the Fugitive Slave Act, he penned his memorable essay "On the Duty of Civil Disobedience," published in Elizabeth Peabody's *Aesthetic Papers* in 1849. Of all his work, it has probably had a greater influence on the lives of more people than any other, for Mahatma Gandhi read it early in his struggle for Indian independence and made its thesis of passive resistance to government the keystone of his revolutionary program. Unlike that other influential political document published the year before, Marx's Communist Manifesto, it preached pure philosophic anarchy as the ultimate goal to be achieved not through concerted action but through the individual's withdrawing from the state by refusing to pay taxes, submit to military service, or obey laws that conflict with his own conscience.

"How does it become a man to behave toward this American government today?" asks Thoreau. "I answer, that he cannot without disgrace be associated with it."[28] Thoreau holds that only the individual, not by waiting until he has persuaded a majority to alter unjust laws, but by at once withdrawing from his copartnership with the state can effect the reform of government. If imprisonment is to be the penalty imposed, then "under a government which imprisons any unjustly, the true place for a just man is also a prison."[29] If men would act so, then progress toward "a more perfect and glorious State" that he has imagined but not yet seen would be possible. That state is, of course, theoretical anarchy, in which each man is the wise governor of himself, acting with respect for the rights and interests of his neighbors.

After reading "Civil Disobedience," one can understand why Thoreau had such a profound admiration for John Brown. Brown's defiance of the "orderly" processes of government in behalf of his belief that slavery must be ended not tomorrow but today was the embodiment of Thoreau's thesis. So great was his enthusiasm for Brown that he likened him to Jesus, that other great revolutionary spirit in the cause of human freedom. And, as Harding has pointed out, the highest praise he gave Brown was to think of him as a Transcendentalist, one who followed the dictates of the voice within even though it conflicted with the policies of the government.[30] In his "The Last Days of John Brown," he noted in the following significant words the change in public opinion that came over the North after the pronouncement of Brown's death sentence: "The North, I mean the *living* North, was suddenly all transcendental. It went behind the human law, it went behind the apparent failure, and recognized eternal justice and glory. Commonly, men live according to a formula, and are satisfied if the order of law is observed, but in this instance they, to some extent, returned to original perceptions, and there was a slight revival of old religion."[31]

Thoreau, of course, has been accused of inconsistency in glorifying Brown, who chose the un-Thoreauvian course of violence and bloodshed rather than passive resistance in his opposition to the laws that he would not obey. It was not, however, Brown's violence that Thoreau applauded, but rather his unswerving pursuit of a course of action designed to carry out his belief in the great principle that no man should be compelled to be a slave.

Of all Thoreau's published writings, it is "Life Without Principle," the revised lecture on making a living, that most forthrightly states the Transcendentalist position on the prevailing materialistic attitude in the United States. In it Thoreau mounts his heaviest siege guns against the getting and spending that occupy the attention of his fellow Americans almost to the exclusion of all else. "I think," he says, "that there is nothing, not even crime, more opposed to poetry, to philosophy, ay, to life itself, than this incessant business."[32] For the primary aim of business is the making of money, and "the ways by which you may get money almost without exception lead downward."[33] The services that society is most willing to pay for are those that he finds most disagreeable to render; the community, however, "has no bribe that will tempt a wise man."[34] The secret of getting a satisfactory living is to love the work you do; thus it is no longer work, but pleasure. He sees himself as more than usually jealous about his freedom; therefore, to insure that he does not have to sell much of his time to society, he has chosen to simplify his needs. Time being the most valuable of commodities, the more of it one has to do with as he wishes, the richer he is. He concludes, "There is no more fatal blunderer than he who consumes the greater part of his life getting his living. All great enterprises are self-supporting."[35]

Emerson had once remarked of his young friend, "How comic is simplicity in this doubledealing quacking world. Everything that boy says makes merry with society though nothing can be graver than his message."[36] No one has judged Thoreau more shrewdly.

CHAPTER 7

Whitman

W HEN Charles Eliot Norton hailed Whitman's *Leaves of Grass* upon its publication in 1855 as harmoniously fusing "Yankee transcendentalism and New York rowdyism," he was essentially correct.[1] What his remark implies is that the core of Whitman's thought as embodied in the poems is as transcendental as anything to be found in the writings of the self-acknowledged New England Transcendentalists, but that the language he expressed it in was the easy-gaited, idiomatic diction of his New York environment rather than the relatively cold and academic English of the New England Harvard graduate. What it also implies is that Whitman had charged his poetry with a liberal infusion of sex in a way far more direct than would have been possible for any of the New England group. As we have noted in our chapter on Thoreau, he gave greater vent to the sexual instinct than did Emerson; but its emergence in his writing is indirect, symbolic, often seemingly unconscious. Whitman, however, employed sex as a theme deliberately and directly in keeping with a theory of art and of life that he was at pains to express in the prefaces to the various editions of *Leaves of Grass*. For him, the sexual urge, the urge toward procreation, lay at the base of all art as well as all life. Unfortunately, it had been suppressed in his time as something vile, to be hidden rather than celebrated. But he, Walt Whitman, would restore sex to its proper place as the equal of spirit. Body and soul, the physical and the spiritual— these are counterparts, each entitled to be revered and celebrated without shame but rather with delight.

I am the poet of the Body;
And I am the poet of the Soul.[2]

I believe in the flesh and the appetites;

Seeing, hearing, feeling, are miracles, and each part and tag of me is a
    miracle.
Divine am I inside and out, and I make holy whatever I touch or am
    touch'd from;
The scent of these arm-pits, aroma finer than prayer;
This head more than churches, bibles, and all the creeds.[3]

Although the emphasis on the physical is alien to the New
Englanders, this is genuine Transcendental doctrine. The idea of
the individual man as possessed of divinity, of receiving the divine impulse directly rather than through the mediation of religious institutions, is at one with the message of the young Unitarian reformers who surrounded Emerson. Further, as Conner
has shown, Whitman looked on the world as an aggregation of living entities compounded like himself of body and soul.[4] The soul
or spirit is the molding cause and the body or matter that which
is molded.

Leaves of Grass, like all great books, reflects numerous influences that went into its making, but again like all great books, it
makes astonishingly original use of its source materials. As Allen
has said, ". . .it was Whitman's great achievement to fuse 'hints'
from hundreds of books with the authentic product of his own
fantasy."[5] That one of the most important of these books was
Emerson's *Essays* is scarcely questionable. Although Whitman in
later years tended to play down influences on his work, he had
earlier acknowledged taking the *Essays* with him in his lunch pail
during the months when *Leaves of Grass* was gestating. And the
ideas and spirit of *Nature* and "Self-Reliance" reverberate through
the pages of the younger poet's book. Does Emerson in "The
American Scholar" say that he had better never see a book than
to be warped out of his own orbit by it? Very well, then Whitman says:

Houses and rooms are full of perfumes—the shelves are crowded with
    perfumes;
I breathe the fragrance myself, and know it and like it;
The distillation would intoxicate me also, but I shall not let it.[6]

Or does Emerson in "Self-Reliance" aver that "With consistency a great soul has simply nothing to do"? Whitman puts it
thus:

Do I contradict myself?
Very well, then, I contradict myself,
(I am large—I contain multitudes.)[7]

These seeming echoes of Emerson can be multiplied a hun-
dredfold, but Whitman always expresses the ideas in his own
way, even more so than Emerson had done in his borrowings.
Nor can one deny that Whitman may have arrived quite independently at many of the thoughts he shared with the New England advocates of the Newness. Rufus Jones, for example, has
rightly included him among the mystics, who reach their conclu-
sions intuitively rather than through the analysis of knowledge as
do the rationalists.[8] This fact alone aligns him closely with the
Transcendental Movement.

It is worth remembering that, after receiving from Whitman a
copy of the first edition of *Leaves of Grass*, Emerson dashed off
an enthusiastic letter to the Brooklyn poet greeting him at the
beginning of a great career. Plainly he felt in the first flush of his
rapture that here was the American poet he had been vainly
searching for as described in his essay "The Poet." Here was the
genius "with tyrannous eye" who "knew the value of our incom-
parable materials" and in whose eyes America was a poem. Here
was a poet who embraced the common, the familiar, the low,
who knew the meaning of "the meal in the firkin; the milk in the
pan; the ballad in the street; the news of the boat; the glance of
the eye; the form and the gait of the body. . ."[9] That Emerson's
ardor cooled somewhat later matters little. His spontaneous response is the one that he himself would have had to admit mat
ters most. That Whitman used his letter for advertising purposes
Emerson found embarrassing. That Whitman's taste was questionable in portraying sexuality so openly he could not help pointing out on the occasions when he tried to persuade Whitman to
remove the offending matter from the book. That Whitman refused to take his advice may have been what convinced him not
to include even a single line from *Leaves of Grass* in his 1872
anthology, *Parnassus*. But none of these withdrawals can cancel
out that first honest response to the unexpected note struck by
the unknown New Yorker.

So impressed, indeed, were Emerson and several of his close
friends, that visits were made to New York to search out the new

poet. Alcott and Thoreau were among the first of the emissaries
from New England. Several times they met with Whitman, either
at his home or elsewhere. They were impressed. Despite feeling
him vain, Alcott enjoyed Whitman tremendously but felt that he
and Thoreau were suspicious of each other. But, as Allen points
out, "Thoreau and Whitman were temperamentally so different
that it is surprising they got along as well as they did. But despite
Alcott's impression that they did not trust each other, each had a
simplicity and frankness that the other respected."[10] Then came
Emerson himself, initiating what was to become a series of meetings between the two men which, however, never seemed to
bring them any closer together than they had been when Emerson penned his thrilling letter of discovery.

A close reading of *Leaves of Grass* discloses surely the Transcendental currents that course through the book and lie at its
very foundation. Opening it almost at random, one may find illustrations. Let us look, for instance, at two passages from "Song
of the Open Road" that encompass a number of the most important concepts of the Transcendentalists:

From this hour, freedom!
From this hour I ordain myself loos'd of limits and imaginary lives,
Going where I list, my own master, total and absolute,
Listening to others, and considering well what they say,
Pausing, searching, receiving, contemplating,
Gently, but with undeniable will, divesting myself of the holds that
    would hold me.[11]

Here we see the poet dedicating himself to the concept of individual freedom as forthrightly as ever Thoreau did, to the independence of the self from all authority imposed from without, to
the search for truth wherever it may lead, to the throwing off by
an effort of the will of all bonds that restrain—all perfectly in line
with the Transcendentalists' attitude.

Then again,

Now I see the secret of the making of the best persons,
It is to grow in the open air, and to eat and sleep with the earth.
Here a great personal deed has room;
A great deed seizes upon the hearts of the whole race of men,
Its effusion of strength and will overwhelms law, and mocks all authority
    and all argument against it.

Here is the test of wisdom;
Wisdom is not finally tested in schools;
Wisdom cannot be pass'd from one having it, to another not having it;
Wisdom is of the Soul, is not susceptible of proof, is its own proof,
Applies to all stages and objects and qualities, and is content,
Is the certainty of the reality and immortality of things, and the excel-
    lence of things;
Something there is in the float of the sight of things that provokes it out
    of the Soul.[12]

    In the foregoing passage we find other familiar Transcendental
themes: the necessity of a close contact with nature in order to
bring out the best qualities in the individual; the impotence of
institutional authority in the face of the great-hearted individual's
spontaneous action; the idea that wisdom or truth cannot be im-
parted or proved through logical analysis but is arrived at intuitively through the soul or divine element in man, which alone
provides us with the insight to reality and the timeless good of all
that has been created; finally, the idea that the physical senses
acted on by nature lead one to truth by stimulating the soul.
    Whitman also importantly reveals in statement after statement
the Transcendental sense of what Conner calls "cosmic optimism," the major premise of which was that "the universe is not
alien to man but the embodiment or reflection or prototype of his
own deepest self; because this is the case, the conclusion then follows, the universe *must* aspire toward the same ends as man."[13]
    The 1860 poem "Kosmos" is perhaps the most unified state-
ment of the idea.

Who includes diversity, and is Nature,
Who is the amplitude of the earth, and the coarseness and sexuality of
    the earth, and the great charity of the earth, and the equilibrium
    also,
Who has not look'd forth from the windows, the eyes, for nothing, or
    whose brain held audience with messengers for nothing;
Who contains believers and disbelievers—who is the most majestic lover;
Who holds duly his or her triune proportion of realism, spiritualism, and
    of the aesthetic, or intellectual,
Who, having consider'd the Body, finds all its organs and parts good;
Who, out of the theory of the earth, and of his or her body, understands
    by subtle analogies all other theories,
The theory of a city, a poem, and of the large politics of these States;

Who believes not only in our globe, with its sun and moon, but in other
    globes, with their suns and moons;
Who, constructing the house of himself or herself, not for a day, but for
    all time, sees races, eras, dates, generations,
The past, the future, dwelling there, like space, inseparable together.

Whitman's belief in and devotion to democracy was another aspect of his outlook on life that aligned him with the
Transcendentalists.[14] Not only does *Leaves of Grass* express in a
variety of ways his veneration of the democratic spirit, but such a
detailed prose statement as *Democratic Vistas* of 1871 speaks elo-
quently of his faith that the great American democracy will have
the strength to overcome the forces of corruption in business and
politics that have threatened it. But if we are to be saved, it will
be the poets who will save us. They are to be the seers, the
prophets of the true democratic state, replacing the priests and
the lawgivers who have dominated our institutions in the past.
Here Whitman sees, as did Emerson, the liberating role of the
poet. Only through the enlightenment provided by the poet, who
is the interpreter of God through nature, can men come to see
the truth clearly with their own eyes.

Whitman is also very much at one with the major Transcendentalists in his aesthetic theory. Emerson in "The Poet" struck most
forcefully the note that substance rather than form makes a poem,
going so far as to suggest that, given the substance, the form will
take care of itself. His own poetry progressively reveals a deliberate retreat from conventional forms, meters, and rhyme schemes,
so much so as to make it at times a forerunner of free verse.
Whitman seized upon the freedom from prosodic restrictions
generally espoused if not practiced by the poetically inclined
Transcendentalists to develop the loose, rhythmic, free-striding
style that was to become the most important influence on the development of modern verse. Throwing metrical schemes, rhyme,
and historical verse forms into the discard, he wrote with a varia-
tion of line length within a single poem that made many of his
early critics mistake his verse for prose. His vocabulary was also
frequently and consciously remote from so-called "poetic diction."
The language of the street and the workyard, admired if not emu-
lated by Emerson and his circle, became a staple with Whitman,
who was the first major American poet to write in what Mencken
was to glorify as the American language.

The need of the artist to plunge the self into the universal being is another of the Transcendental aesthetic tenets with which Whitman was in agreement. That a divine unity pervades all art and all life is a persistent theme in *Leaves of Grass*. All things are manifestations, each in its own right, of the overarching One. Thus the self is constantly being identified with all else that exists, Whitman providing example after example of the great Transcendental thesis of unity through variety, and of the individual as microcosm. Thus he will identify with the prostitute, the felon, the idiot, the worm, and the rock; for each and all are part of the divine one, and he must accept them therefore as part of himself.

In the prefaces Whitman insists on the religious element that lies behind his poems, the essential moral purpose that pervades them. We are reminded of John S. Dwight's masterful pronouncement of the Transcendental aesthetic in which he insists that all art is the creation of beauty in the service of expressing a moral end, a meaning of some sort, a something that relates it to the inner or spiritual life of man. That everything without exception has an eternal soul through being a manifestation of what Emerson called the over-soul is the religious meaning that Whitman continually explored in his profuse variety of ways.

Finally, the idea that great art reflects reality is completely accepted and advocated by Whitman. Unlike Poe, who rejected science as the natural enemy of poetry (see his "Sonnet to Science"), he welcomes the exact scientist as a lawgiver to the poet. The scientist, who searches for truth (reality), provides an ever more accurate picture of what really is, thereby expanding rather than contracting the horizons of the poet, whom he provides with an always strengthening foundation of reality on which to build his poetic visions:

Hurrah for positive science! long live exact demonstration!
. . . .
Gentlemen! to you the first honors always:
Your facts are useful and real—and yet they are not my dwelling;
(I but enter by them to an area of my dwelling.)[15]

CHAPTER 8

Some Other Important
Transcendentalists

ALTHOUGH Emerson, Thoreau, and Whitman have made the
most enduring mark as literary figures among those who may
properly be called Transcendentalists, they were only three
among many who made significant contributions to the movement. Because of the present importance of those three to
American literature it has seemed appropriate to devote a chapter
to each. In this chapter the attempt will be made to present in
brief compass the achievement of a number of others whose
names can never be forgotten in any history of American Transcendentalism.

A perhaps inevitable figure to begin with is Amos Bronson Alcott (1799–1888), for many years Emerson's close friend and in so
many respects the seeming embodiment of the Transcendental
spirit. His principal biographer, Odell Shepard, has defined him
as being an idealist before he had read a word of Plato and a
Transcendentalist before he had heard the name of Emerson.[1]
Coming from a background of virtual poverty in rural Connecticut, Alcott had little formal education. His five journeys into the
South as a peddler between 1818 and 1822 taught him more, he
said, than any college could have.[2] And his travels among the
Quakers of North Carolina particularly helped him "to take his
first long step toward transcendentalism."[3] Later, he taught country school in Connecticut, introducing such novel ideas as the
honor system, organized play, and the sparing of the rod. He
conducted his own schools in Boston and Germantown, Pennsylvania, before opening in 1834 his famous Temple School in Boston. With the assistance of such stalwart women as Elizabeth
Peabody and Margaret Fuller, he gave free rein to his educa-

tional theories, appealing to the intellectual faculties of his pupils
by introducing the discussion method and by instituting a series
of "Conversations on the Gospels." In these his primary purpose
seems to have been to use the children as divining rods for ex-
ploring the true meaning of the New Testament so that that meaning might be apprehended by adults. Rejecting historical scholarship as useless, he embraced the Transcendental proposition
that in children natural intuition is most reliable; ergo, their fresh
reaction to the biblical text would establish its truth.[4] Publication
in 1836 and 1837 of the record of these conversations brought
down on Alcott's head a storm of abuse from press and public
that quite bewildered him. Conservative Boston accused him, in
brief, of corrupting the young minds entrusted to his care, and
even the efforts of his more liberal friends could not save him or
his school from the effect of these attacks. Enrollment fell
sharply, and by 1839 Alcott was obliged to sell the physical assets
of the school to pay his mounting debts.

Although the Temple School came to this unhappy close, the
idea behind it survived. J.P. Greaves in England, for example,
named his school near London "Alcott House" after Harriet Mar-
tineau had acquainted him with the record of Alcott's achievement at the Temple School.[5]

Alcott's brand of Transcendentalism disposed him unfavorably
toward Kant's philosophy, which he viewed as pedestrian and
sensual. Classing Kant with Aristotle, Bacon, and Locke as nar-
rowers of the range of human faculties, Alcott claimed that he,
like those others, shut up the soul in the cave of the
understanding.[6] His own attitudes were most vividly expressed in
a series of epigrams, the "Orphic Sayings," first published in *The
Dial* for July, 1840. Regarded as pretentious nonsense by most of
those who read them, they served neither to enhance Alcott's
reputation nor that of the magazine. The reader of a later day can
see perhaps more readily that it was, in Frothingham's words,
"the mystic phrase, and the perpetual reiteration of absolute
principles that made the propositions seem obscure."[7]

We have discussed in an earlier chapter Alcott's idealistic
Fruitlands experiment in communal living that ended so disas-
trously and shall say nothing further about it here. It need only be
added that Alcott was not always doomed to failure or to ridicule.
He enjoyed a triumphal London visit in 1842 subsidized by

Emerson and other friends; he performed admirably after 1859 as superintendent of the Concord public school system; and in 1879 he presided with distinction over the Concord School of Philosophy. Granted a certain impracticality in worldly affairs, which even his family were quick to recognize, Alcott was perhaps the quintessential Transcendentalist, great in heart, lofty in spirit, and unflinching in optimism until the day he died.

A more gifted writer and more brilliant theoretician than Alcott was Orestes A. Brownson (1803–1876). Like Alcott, he was raised in near poverty on a farm and had no formal schooling. Eager for religious experience, he ran the gamut from the hardbacked Calvinism of New England through Presbyterianism, Universalism, Unitarianism, Transcendentalism, and finally Roman Catholicism, to which he was converted in 1844, much to the regret of those who had come to look on him as a firebrand of the Transcendental cause. For the ten years before that date his pen, first in the columns of *The Christian Examiner*, then in his own *Boston Quarterly Review*, had been the most dauntless defender of the Transcendentalist belief, the most feared opponent of those who would demean it. Although sharing the common enthusiasm for Coleridge and Carlyle felt by the disciples of the Newness, his particular idol was the French eclectic philosopher Victor Cousin, of whose work he was the most ardent apostle in America.

To read Brownson at his best one might well turn to his stirring defense of Transcendentalism against the charge of infidelity made by the redoubtable Andrews Norton. It appeared in the July, 1840, issue of *The Boston Quarterly Review* under the title "Two Articles from *The Princeton Review*." Referring to the Transcendental Movement, he termed it a revolution extending to every department of thought and threatening to "change ultimately the whole moral aspect of our society." Pointing to the impact already made, he expressed the certainty that "the revolution—or movement, if the term be preferred,—has already extended too far to be arrested, and is so radical in its nature, that none who take the least interest in the general condition of their race, can regard it with indifference."[8]

"The real aim of the Transcendentalist," declared Brownson, "is to ascertain a solid ground for faith in the reality of the spiritual world."[9] But he expressed with a greater clarity and directness than anyone else had the wide differences of opinion existing among the members of the movement, holding that they agreed in little except

> their common opposition to the old school. . . . Some of them embrace the Transcendental philosophy, some of them reject it, some of them *ignore* all philosophy, plant themselves on their instincts, and wait for the huge world to come round to them. Some of them read Cousin, some Goethe and Carlyle, others none at all. Some of them reason, others merely dream. No single term can describe them. Nothing can be more unjust to them, or more likely to mislead the public than to lump them all together, and predicate the same things of them all.[10]

Brownson himself, although one of the original members of the Transcendental Club, was as different in attitude from an Emerson or a Parker as could be. As Miller has pointed out, they took the principles of the new philosophy as a promise of indefinite enlargements of individual freedom, whereas he took them as a promise of organic authority.[11] He himself, in his autobiography, *The Convert*, acknowledged the uncertainty of his convictions and the extravagant and paradoxical nature of much of his writing. His intention was to be a gadfly to his countrymen's mental activity by forcing them to think independently on the gravest subjects. In this he was largely successful; however, it is necessary in the final analysis to agree with Frothingham's conclusion that his writings were ephemeral, their interest largely ceasing with the events that inspired them.[12]

Brownson's close friend, George Ripley (1802–1880), of whom we have already written in connection with his calling the first meeting of the Transcendental Club and his founding of the Brook Farm Association, was surely one of the most diligent, energetic, and altruistic members of the movement. As dedicated to principle as Emerson, he too resigned an important Unitarian pulpit when he found that not to do so would conflict with his beliefs.[13] A brilliant Harvard scholar, he read widely and in 1838 began publishing in Boston one of the most valuable of Transcendental enterprises, *Specimens of Foreign Standard Literature*, which brought to American readers the new literature of the European continent in a series of scholarly translations by various members of the movement. For example, Margaret Fuller translated Eckermann's *Conversations*, W.H. Channing the philosophy of Jouffroy, and Dwight selections from Goethe and Schiller.

As early as 1832 Ripley began publishing in *The Christian Examiner* essays that anticipated the full flowering of the Transcendentalist revolt against materialism, but it is with Brook Farm that his name will always be primarily associated. He and his wife Sophia quite literally gave their blood, sweat, and tears to the enterprise, whose failure in 1847 left them bereft. Although serving with distinction in succeeding Margaret Fuller as the New York *Tribune's* literary critic, Ripley never again was a factor in the movement. But in 1845 he had written a declaration of policy for his new journal, *The Harbinger*, that stated with unmistakable clarity the doctrine of those Transcendentalists who found in the movement the opportunity to remake society by reforming its institutions. "The interests of Social Reform," he wrote, "will be considered as paramount to all others, in whatever is admitted into the pages of the Harbinger. We shall suffer no attachment to literature, no taste for abstract discussion, no love of purely intellectual theories, to seduce us from our devotion to the cause of the oppressed, the down trodden, the insulted and injured masses of our fellow men."[14] Not even a Parrington could say it better in a later day.

Perhaps of equal importance with the essays of Brownson and Ripley in *The Christian Examiner* were those of Frederic Henry Hedge (1805–1890), at least insofar as they helped to establish the Transcendental Movement. His article on Coleridge in the *Examiner* for March, 1833, provided the first American recognition of the claims of transcendentalism. He defined it as "not a skeptical philosophy; it seeks not to overthrow, but to build up; it wars not with the common opinions and general experience of mankind, but aims to place these on a scientific basis, and to verify them by scientific demonstrations."[15] Stressing the importance of free intuition attained only "by a vigorous effort of the will," he claimed that it was "from an ignorance of this primary condition" that the writings of Kant and his followers had been denounced "as vague and mystical."[16]

For Hedge, son of a Harvard professor, graduate of Harvard in 1825 and of its Divinity School in 1829, and pastor of Unitarian churches in West Cambridge, Bangor, and Brookline, Transcendentalism offered an avenue for opposing the rise of evangelical and "unenlightened" orthodoxy. Like such men as James Marsh, Congregationalist minister, professor of Oriental languages at

Hampden-Sidney College, president of the University of Vermont, and professor of philosophy there, and Caleb Sprague Henry, Congregationalist minister and then Episcopalian priest as well as professor of mental and moral philosophy at New York University, Hedge centered his interest and work in the Christian church. In this important respect they differed from such Transcendental leaders as Emerson and Ripley, who found their ministries incompatible with their vision of individual freedom.

For Hedge, Marsh, and Henry a constructive substitute for Calvinist orthodoxy was the primary need. Thus they saw Transcendentalism as "not primarily a theory of knowledge or a system of ethics, but an assertion of religious faith that was neither derived from natural science and natural rights and in that sense transcendental nor dependent upon ecclesiastical tradition and in that sense philosophical."[17] All three opposed the Lockean idea that reason is demonstrative and discursive. For all of them, reason and reflection lead to "living" rather than to "logical" truth, "living" because spiritual and moral truth is seen as part of man's active nature. The practical consequence for Marsh was the lively contemplation of the living God; for Henry and Hedge it was moral reforms and humanitarian love. All three championed science as valid and acceptable to the church and did not repudiate this aspect of the Enlightenment; all three also agreed that the starting point for philosophy and religion is "the divine root in man," "our proper humanity."[18] Hedge as well as Henry emphasized the social aspects of the Gospel, and Hedge was especially active in transforming the humanitarian Gospel of Dr. Channing into a more radical gospel of social reform.[19]

Hedge's career in the Unitarian church was capped by his editorship of *The Christian Examiner* from 1857 to 1861 and his presidency of the Unitarian Association from 1859 to 1862. He was also a remarkable teacher and held professorships at Harvard in ecclesiastical history in the Divinity School (1857–1876) and in German literature in the College (1872–1884). His 1865 book, *Reason in Religion*, remains the classic statement of Transcendental Christianity.

Another of the charter members of Hedge's Club (Emerson's playful term for the Transcendental Club) to perform yeoman service in the spreading of the Transcendental ideals was James Freeman Clarke (1810–1888), another graduate of Harvard and its

Divinity School, who went west with a group of Harvard friends intent on extending the culture and the Unitarianism of New England to such benighted communities as Cincinnati and Louisville. The magazine Clarke edited from 1836 to 1839, *The Western Messenger*, was their main instrument.

Like Hedge, Marsh and Henry, Clarke insisted always that he was a Christian as well as a Transcendentalist; but unlike some of the other members of the movement, he remained a staunch defender of the Transcendental faith until the end. His posthumously published *Autobiography* describes well the kind of inner experience most of the members must have undergone. Speaking of his early acquaintance with "the polemic of Locke against innate ideas," he says, "something within me revolted at all such attempts to explain soul out of sense, deducing mind from matter, or tracing the origin of ideas to nerves, vibrations, and vibratiuncles. So I concluded I had no taste for metaphysics and gave it up, until Coleridge showed me from Kant that though knowledge begins *with* experience it does not come *from* experience. Then I discovered that I was born a transcendentalist. . . ."[20]

The man who, in the words of Perry Miller, "next only to Emerson—and in the world of action even above Emerson—was to give shape and meaning to the Transcendental movement in America"[21] was Theodore Parker (1810–1860), a poor New England farmer's son who had little formal schooling but who read voraciously. Admitted to Harvard, he lacked the tuition fees to attend classes but nonetheless passed the examinations; conducted a school for a time; went for two years to Harvard Divinity School; accepted a pulpit in West Roxbury; and became a close friend of Ripley and Brownson. A prodigious scholar, he had mastered no fewer than twenty languages.

Possessing a natural gift for powerful speech, Parker was an unusually persuasive preacher who was also able to transfer much of the flavor of his speech to the printed page in the form of articles and essays that are models of clear thought and direct expression.

His best biographer, Henry Steele Commager, shows us that Parker's view of the Christian church and his basic reason for remaining within it was that it should be and could be the means of reforming the world after the pattern of Christian ideals. Commager has written that with every year he grew more radical in his thinking and bolder in his action. The Peace Society of Massachusetts was organized in his study; and in his study, too, Dorothea Dix prepared her moving Memorial on the condition of the insane. He championed penal reform and the abolition of capital punishment, and assured his wealthy parishioners that the criminal caught the infection of vice from the upper classes. He was among the first to celebrate the work of Horace Mann, and he urged the president of Harvard College to provide democratic education for the plain people of the country.[22]

Schneider has remarked that Parker's transcendentalism was more critical than romantic[23] and sees him as one who "understood better than any of his American contemporaries how to interpret the critical philosophy of Kant as a flowering of the Enlightenment. . . ."[24] Indeed Schneider sees Parker as following Kant "in emphasizing morality or 'practical holiness' as the most important part of religion."[25]

Typical of the kind of ferment Parker was accustomed to cause was his sermon of May 19, 1841, which he had been invited to give in connection with the ordination of Charles C. Shackford in the South Boston Church. Entitled "A Discourse of the Transient and Permanent in Christianity," it created a furor that resulted in Parker's being all but ostracized by respectable Boston. Other ministers would no longer exchange pulpits with him and few refused to condemn him. His own congregation, however, stood by him. And what was it that so outraged the conservative Unitarians of Boston? It was Parker's attack on historical Christianity and the idolatry accorded Scripture:

Current notions respecting the infallible inspiration of the Bible have no foundation in the Bible itself. Which evangelist, which apostle of the New Testament, what prophet or psalmist of the Old Testament, ever claims infallible authority for himself or for others? Which of them does not in his own writings show that he was finite, and, with all his zeal and piety, possessed but a limited inspiration, the bound whereof we can sometimes discover?[26]

Thus did he assail the traditional assumption that all of the authors of Scripture were infallibly and miraculously inspired so that they could commit no error of doctrine or fact.

A member of the Transcendental Club and an admirer of Emerson, Parker in a letter to Emerson of October 11, 1853, attempted to revive the long defunct club, but no meeting was ever again called.[27] Emerson's own respect for Parker's logical mind and skill in argument is perhaps best attested by his oft-quoted remark in reporting a debate between Alcott and Parker, that Parker "wound himself around Alcott like an anaconda; you could hear poor Alcott's bones crunch." Nonetheless Emerson could never quite warm to Parker's "logical, sledge-hammer mind."[28]

When he knew in 1859 that he was soon to die, Parker wrote a farewell letter to his church, eventually published under the title *Theodore Parker's Experience as a Minister*, in which he summed up the foundation of religion as he saw it, a foundation which is thoroughly Transcendental. He mentions the three great primal intuitions of human nature that pertain to religion:

"1. The instinctive intuition of the divine, the consciousness that there is a God.

"2. The instinctive intuition of the just and right, a consciousness that there is a moral law, independent of our will, which we ought to keep.

"3. The instructive intuition of the immortal, a consciousness that the essential element of man, the principle of individuality, never dies."[29]

Commager has perhaps paid Parker his greatest tribute in the simple statement, "He knew that reason would triumph over unreason."[30]

Perhaps the handsomest and surely the most amusing of the Transcendentalists was Parker's fellow student at the Harvard Divinity School, Christopher Pearse Cranch (1813–1892). A graduate of Columbian College (now George Washington University) in 1832, he entered the ministry in 1835 after his stint at Harvard. Preaching as a missionary at large for the Unitarian Association, he never had a pulpit of his own. Following Clarke to the West, he became an editor of *The Western Messenger*, to which he contributed both prose and verse. His reading at the age of twenty-three of *Nature* and *Sartor Resartus* apparently lit the Transcendental flame in him. Taking note in an article in the *Messenger* of January, 1841, of the then current attacks on Transcendentalism as, in Norton's words, "the latest form of infidelity," he found it amusing "to see how Kant, Cousin, Carlyle, Emerson, and about half Germany, are placed side by side, as if reading like schoolboys, out of the same book. . . ."[31] Indeed he saw Transcendentalism in rhapsodic terms as "that fresh, earnest, truth-loving and truth-seeking SPIRIT, which is abroad. . . something always adapted to the soul's deep demands."[32]

A friend of almost all the better known Transcendentalists, Cranch wrote frequently for *The Dial* and eventually became known for his gently satirical cartoons of Emerson and others. In later life he became a landscape painter, one of the less distinguished of the Hudson River School.

If Cranch turned out to be something of a dilettante, Jones Very (1813–1880), born in the same year, most certainly did not. The son of a Salem sea captain, he was graduated from Harvard in 1836, was made tutor in Greek there, and also entered the Divinity School. Almost immediately he began to have visions and to receive, he claimed, commands from the Holy Ghost. Asked in 1838 to resign from the Harvard faculty on the grounds of possible insanity, he spent several weeks in an asylum before being released as probably cured.

To Emerson, Very was the "vibrant personification of transcendental humanity, a partaker of Universal Reason, a sharer in the Over-Soul. He, more than any other of his contemporaries, seemed to Emerson to rely on intuition, and not on history or social customs as a source of truth."[33] Thus Emerson encouraged the young man with his sonnets, which, however, Very insisted were dictated directly to him by God. But it was Elizabeth Peabody who decided in 1837 that he should be the poet of the Transcendental School,[34] and it was she who introduced him to Emerson, who in 1839 managed the publication of his *Essays and Poems* after doing a job of selection and revision. In the same year Clarke published twenty-seven of the poems in his *Western Messenger*. Emerson's words in "The Poet," "If a man is inflamed and carried away by his thought, to that degree that he forgets the authors and the public and needs only this one dream which holds him like an insanity, let me read his paper. . ."[35] apply more fully to Very than to any other poet of the movement with the possible exception of Whitman, who, however, seems to have been more deliberate than Very in his creative process. But after 1840 Very's religious ecstasy began to subside and his poetry was

reduced to the level of technically adequate verse. The last forty
years of his life were spent in seclusion in Salem, the candle of
his creativity apparently burned out.[36]

Quite probably because the Transcendental Movement was so
much a movement of reform and liberality, it welcomed the participation of women on equal terms with their brethren. In consequence, although women scarcely came to dominate the
movement, many of them played significant roles and at least
two, through the force of their personalities and the keenness of
their intellects, contributed inestimably. They were Elizabeth
Peabody (1804–1894) and Margaret Fuller (1810–1850).

Both Elizabeth and her sister Sophia, who married Hawthorne,
were ardent Transcendentalists,[37] but Elizabeth, a lifelong spin-
ster, was able to devote herself more single-mindedly to the
cause. As the friend and secretary of the great Dr. Channing she
was well placed to meet the most brilliant young minds in Boston. Among them was Alcott, whom she early recognized as a
superb teacher. Introducing him to Dr. Channing, she secured
the latter's approval for the idea of the Temple School, which she
helped Alcott to open in 1834. And it was she who published in
1835 her remarkable *Record of Mr. Alcott's School* in which she
preserved for posterity a precise, often stenographic account of
Alcott's experiment in Transcendental education.

In 1839 the indefatigable Miss Peabody opened in her father's
home in West Street a bookshop that soon became the meeting-
place for the disciples of the Newness. Emerson, Dwight, Ripley,
Alcott, Hedge, Hawthorne, Margaret Fuller and many another of
the new intelligentsia might be found there on any given after-
noon. And it was there that she undertook to publish *The Dial* as
the prime literary organ of the Transcendental Movement, and
later the short-lived but important *Aesthetic Papers*.

Although she wrote much, including valuable reminiscences of
Dr. Channing and the painter Washington Allston, as well as text-
books on grammar and history, it was as a living spark or catalyst
for Transcendental reform that she had her principal effect. Much
as Sylvia Beach almost a century later at her Paris bookstore,
Shakespeare & Company, served to bring such literati as Joyce,
Eliot, Pound, Hemingway, and Ford together in a congenial atmosphere so did she manage to set the Transcendental sparks fly-
ing. It was at the West Street shop, for example, that the Brook
Farm idea was discussed months before it became a reality. And

it was there that shares in Dr. Ripley's Utopian community were sold.

Among Miss Peabody's other contributions was the sponsorship at the West Street house in 1839 of Margaret Fuller's "Conversations," held periodically until 1844. The daughter of a stern Newburyport Congressman, Margaret received at his insistence an education that made her, in the words of Perry Miller, "the most learned woman in America."[38] Desirous of sharing her thoughts and her learning, she hit upon the idea, probably inspired by Alcott's example, of holding a series of conversations, as she called them, with interested persons on a wide variety of subjects. And although Frothingham declares that "strictly speaking, she was not a Transcendentalist"[39] but was predominantly a critic, her enthusiasm and effort in behalf of the movement are unquestionable. ". . .I sympathize with what is called the 'Transcendental Party,' " she said, "and. . .I feel their aim to be the true one. They acknowledge in the nature of man an arbiter for his deeds—a standard transcending sense and time—and are, in my view, the true utilitarians."[40]

In common with Emerson, Margaret Fuller believed that genius would be no rare commodity if men and women were to trust their higher selves. Seeking out the boldest minds of her community, she made friends of Clarke, W. H. Channing, Hedge, and even the great Emerson. She assisted Alcott at the Temple School and worked tirelessly to improve her mind and elevate her spirit. Interested in Brook Farm from the beginning, she resisted all entreaties to join in. For her as for Emerson and Thoreau the true path to the reform of society lay in reform of the self. An ardent feminist, she produced a brilliant analysis of the contemporary position of her sex entitled *Woman in the Nineteenth Century.*

Fulfilling a long-felt desire to visit Europe, she arrived there in 1846, met an Italian nobleman, Angelo Ossoli, the next year, married him, and bore a child in 1848. Hawthorne, who had known her in Concord, could not understand what attraction she found in such a boor as the youthful Ossoli, several years her junior and no match for her intellectually. But then, Hawthorne had always found her lacking in the charm of womanhood. "She was," he wrote,

a person anxious to try all things, and fill up her experience in all direc-

tions; she had a strong and coarse nature, which she had done her ut-
most to refine, with infinite pains; but of course it could only be superficially changed. . . . She was a great humbug—of course, with much tal-
ent and much moral reality, or else she could never have been so great a
humbug. . . . It was such an awful joke, that she should have
resolved. . .to make herself the greatest, wisest, best woman of the age.
And to that end she set to work on her strong, heavy, unpliable, and, in
many respects, defective and evil nature, and adorned it with a mosaic of
admirable qualities, such as she chose to possess. . . .[41]

That other of her Transcendental colleagues did not share
Hawthorne's harsh view of her as a humbug is best shown by the
selfless action of Emerson, W. H. Channing, and Clarke in going
through her papers and selecting the materials for the two volumes of *Memoirs* that they published in 1852, two years after her
tragic death in a shipwreck off Fire Island while she, Ossoli, and
their child were returning to America. The *Memoirs* reveal, as
Frothingham so well expresses it, that "with her, principles were
independent of time and place. She always believed in liberty as
a condition of enlightenment, and in enlightenment as a condition
of progress."[42]

Of all her services to the Transcendental cause quite probably
her two years' editorship of *The Dial* had the greatest long-term
significance. For, in association with Emerson, she set the standards for a critical literature the like of which America had not
yet seen as well as providing a vehicle for the expression of a
wide range of original Transcendental thought, both prose and
poetry. It was, for example, in *The Dial* for July of 1843, under
Emerson's editorship, that her article "The Great Lawsuit," the
initial version of her book on woman, appeared. In it she gave
clear voice to the essentially Transcendentalist doctrine that souls
know no sex and that therefore "every path must be laid open to
women as freely as to man." The immediate practical result of
Margaret Fuller's pioneer work in the cause of women's liberation
was the important Seneca Falls Conference of 1848 on women's
rights.

It should, of course, be stressed that the foregoing figures are
only a few of many who were active in the early stages of the
Transcendental Movement. They have been included primarily
because, through their writings, they have exerted a more enduring influence than have most of their less literary colleagues.

CHAPTER 9

Critics of Transcendentalism

I T is to be expected that any movement of an intellectual, philosophic, or religious character that breaks with an established tradition will evoke strenuous criticism, much of it adverse. The Transcendental Movement was certainly no exception. Almost from the outset it was under attack, and the attack came from various quarters—academic, ecclesiastic, and literary. Even the man in the street expressed his disdain for such nonsense, moving the usually Olympian Emerson to complain plaintively about a piece in a Providence newspaper that took a dim view of Transcendentalism, ". . .cannot society come to apprehend the doctrine of One Mind? . . .How long before *Universalism* or Humanity shall be creditable & beautiful?"[1] As late as 1881, when his *Patience* was produced, W. S. Gilbert, as Hutchison has pointed out, reflected the common man's tendency to confuse Transcendentalism with such other "outlandish" things as the Pre-Raphaelite Brotherhood. Gilbert's lines read:

If you're anxious for to shine in the high aesthetic line, as a man of culture rare,
You must get up all the germs of the Transcendental terms, and plant them everywhere.
You must lie among the daisies and discourse in novel phrases of your complicated state of mind
(The meaning doesn't matter if it's only idle chatter of a transcendental kind). . .
Though the Philistines may jostle, you will rank as an apostle in the high aesthetic band,
If you walk down Picadilly with a poppy or a lily in your medieval hand. . .[2]

To be taken more seriously, however, than the random ambuscades appearing in the popular press were the attacks mounted by respected scholars, leading clergymen, and eminent writers. Among the first to enter the lists against the Transcendentalists were the Harvard scholars Andrews Norton and Francis Bowen.

Norton, a ferocious adversary, had virtually ruled the Divinity School from 1819 to 1830, a time when Emerson, Ripley, Clarke, and Hedge were students there. Even after resigning his office at the school, he continued to dominate the world of Unitarian theology in and about Boston.[3] Growing increasingly irritated with the Transcendentalist view as expressed by Ripley in the pages of the *Christian Examiner* and by Emerson in the newly published *Nature* that man could find religion for himself without supernatural aid or the mediation of the clergy, he turned upon his former students, charging them with "professional and academic incompetence."[4] Declaring that he would no longer participate in editing the *Examiner* if it continued to print articles expressive of Transcendental heresies, he effectively closed the pages of this foremost journal of Unitarianism to the disciples of the Newness, requiring them, in effect, to found their own publications. But it was Emerson's address of July 15, 1838, to the senior class of the Divinity School that elicited Norton's most violent cries of outrage. Instead of using the pages of the *Examiner* for his diatribe, he took the indecorous step of sending his virulent protest against "The New School in Literature and Religion" to *The Boston Daily Advertiser*, which published it in its issue of August 27, 1838.

Warming to his task with an attack on some of the forerunners of American Transcendentalism, he wrote:

The atheist Shelley has been quoted and commended in a professedly religious work, called the Western Messenger; but he is not, we conceive, to be reckoned among the patriarchs of the sect. But this honor is due to that hasher up of German metaphysics, the Frenchman, Cousin; and, of late, that hyper-Germanized Englishman, Carlyle, has been the great object of admiration and model of style. Cousin and Carlyle indeed seem to have been transformed into idols to be publicly worshipped, the former for his philosophy, and the latter both for his philosophy and his fine writing; while the veiled image of the German pantheist, Schleiermacher, is kept in the sanctuary.[5]

The Transcendentalists' characteristics he cited as "the most extraordinary assumption, united with great ignorance, and incapacity for reasoning." He went on to remark of them, "the rejection of reasoning is accompanied with an equal contempt for good taste. All modesty is laid aside." Coming finally to Emerson's address, Norton concludes that "religion has been insulted by the delivery of these opinions" in the form of an "incoherent rhapsody."[6]

The vicious character of this attack on Emerson's address was, it should be noted, unrepresentative of the general Unitarian reaction. Although most Unitarians were in disagreement with the views Emerson had expressed, they were annoyed and embarrassed by the intemperate nature of Norton's remarks, so remote were they from the sober caution that they valued so highly.[7] But Norton was not through. He returned to the offensive with an address of his own at a meeting of the Divinity School alumni on July 19, 1839, entitled "A Discourse on the Latest Form of Infidelity." It was his most memorable production. "The latest form of infidelity," he asserted, "is distinguished by assuming the Christian name, while it strikes directly at the root of faith in Christianity, and indirectly of all religion, by denying the miracles attesting the divine mission of Christ. . . ."[8] Norton concluded by staunchly defending the principle of establishing religious belief through reliance on the knowledge of others whom one regards as intelligent and trustworthy; in other words, *"belief on authority."*[9]

If Norton was intemperate in his criticism, his junior ally, Francis Bowen, was scarcely less so. A Harvard graduate with highest honors in 1833, he became tutor in philosophy at Harvard in 1836 and Alford Professor in 1853. To him the editors of the *Examiner* assigned Emerson's *Nature* for review. In the January, 1837, issue the first part of his critical essay appeared. Although Bowen admitted that there was beautiful writing and sound philosophy in Emerson's "little work," he quickly tied it to the

new school of philosophy. . .the adherents of which have dignified it with the title of Transcendentalism. (He went on to charge that) from the heights of mystical speculation, they look down with a ludicrous self-complacency and pity on the mass of mankind, on the ignorant and the educated, the learners and the teachers, and should any question the grounds on which such feelings rest, they are forthwith branded with the most opprobrious epithets, which the English or the Transcendental language can supply.[10]

The second part of the essay, published in November, 1837, is even less restrained, charging the Transcendentalists with arrogance, un-American Germanness, flippancy, and a strange, fantastical originality. Plainly, war had been declared on Emerson and Company. Ripley, Brownson, and others fought back, sometimes brilliantly as in Ripley's 1839 pamphlet "The Latest Form of Infidelity Examined" which refuted Norton's notion of the importance to religion of scholars like himself. Jesus, Ripley argued, established no college of apostles and paid no special respect to the pride of learning. True learning, he held, is conscious of human frailty and is therefore as modest as it is inquisitive.

Emerson himself remained aloof from the field of combat although at times revealing a certain impatience with the attacks launched on Transcendentalism in general and its new organ of expression, *The Dial*, in particular. In a letter to Carlyle of August 30, 1840, he wrote, "Our community begin to stand in some terror of Transcendentalism, & the Dial, poor little thing, whose first number contains scarce anything considerable or even visible, is just now honoured by attacks from almost every newspaper & magazine; which at least betrays the irritability & the instincts of the good public."[11]

Although academic criticism of both Emerson and Transcendentalism has mellowed with the passage of time, we find such eminent voices as those of George Santayana and James Truslow Adams raised in scholarly protest. Santayana's attitude toward Transcendentalism and its most famous exponent is seen to be at best ambivalent. For example, he saw Emerson's over-soul as nothing more than a philosophic and poetic substitution of a beneficent force for Puritanism's theological providence. Conveniently, it removed both churchgoing and damnation as necessities, while leaving the impulse to worship intact and enhancing its moral fervor.[12]

Joe Lee Davis sees Santayana as rationalizing his ambivalence in his "The Genteel Tradition in American Philosophy" of 1911, from which Davis quotes the following telling passage:

Transcendentalism is systematic subjectivism. It studies the perspectives of knowledge as they radiate from the self; it is a plan of those avenues of inference by which our ideas of things must be reached, if they are to afford any systematic or distant vistas. In other words, transcendentalism is the critical logic of science. . . . Transcendental logic, the method of discovery for the mind, was to become also the method of evolution in nature and history. Transcendental method, so abused, produced transcendental myth. A conscientious critique of knowledge was turned into a sham system of nature. We must therefore distinguish sharply the transcendental grammar of the intellect, which is significant and potentially correct, from the various transcendental systems of the universe, which are chimeras."[13]

Adams, writing in the *Atlantic Monthly* for October, 1930, is more direct and biting. In an essay titled "Emerson Re-Read" he questions the maturity of a Transcendental doctrine that refuses to recognize and to wrestle with the problem of evil. The belief that "knowledge comes from intuition rather than from thought, and that wisdom and goodness are implanted in us" he finds "a fatally easy philosophy." Emerson's influence "shrinks for most of us as we ourselves develop"; for on Adams' close analysis of Emerson's essays, he finds an amazing shallowness, at the bottom of which is an "appalling refusal to criticize, analyze, ponder," a refusal that he holds to be characteristic of the American people themselves.

As for the attitudes toward Transcendentalism of the foremost American literary men outside those who had not admittedly accepted the basic premises of its philosophy, let us take a brief look as they appear at the acme of the movement.

Poe, regarded by Emerson and the New England intellectuals as "the jingle man," was in turn contemptuous of them. Matthiessen refers to his "running fire of satire on the transcendentalists,"[14] while Conner correctly points out that Poe, being attached to the mathematical physical science of the Newtonian tradition, took a corporeal view of reality that was in direct opposition to the idealism of the Transcendentalists. Thus he was "deeply scornful of everything that he recognized as transcendental. . . ."[15] The Transcendental aesthetic was particularly obnoxious to Poe, especially as it applied to poetry. Complaining in "The Poetic Principle" about what he called "the heresy of *The Didactic*," he charged that "it has been assumed, tacitly and avowedly, directly and indirectly, that the ultimate object of all Poetry is Truth. Every poem, it is said, should inculcate a moral. . . . We Americans especially have patronised this happy idea; and we Bostonians, very especially, have developed it in full."[16] Not regarding truth and beauty as synonymous, he held that the only legitimate aim that a poet could have was to create a work of beauty. The Transcendentalist view of art has, then, done more, he feels, to corrupt poetical literature than all its other enemies combined.

For Hawthorne, the difficulty with Transcendentalism was that, although its head was generally in the clouds, it failed more often than not to keep its feet on the ground. As Matthiessen has observed, he "sensed that Emerson's exaltation of the divinity in man had obliterated the distinctions between man and God, between time and eternity." The Christian concept of time, "obscured by Thoreau and Whitman no less than by Emerson in their exhilaration over the fullness of the moment," remained essential to him.[17]

We have seen, in an earlier chapter, that Hawthorne, whose wife worshipped Emerson, knew many of the leading Transcendentalists intimately, and that he went so far as to buy shares in Brook Farm, where he went to live for a time. However, acutely aware of the egotism that sees its own will as inevitably God's will, he became increasingly skeptical of Transcendentalism as being an escape from reality. Thus he could criticize in *The Blithedale Romance* the follies of the quest for Utopia, of the escape from real life to a kind of perpetual garden party, of the failure to recognize the complexity of man's nature. Perhaps it was also that he found people who were so dedicated to reform as were the Transcendentalists to be the least bit boring. After all, he tells us that he used *The Dial* as an agent for putting himself quickly to sleep when he was weary.

Hawthorne's younger neighbor and admirer, Herman Melville, was at least as ambivalent about Transcendentalism as was his sometime idol. Increasingly, however, his stance became adversely critical. Matthiessen, in fact, goes so far as to say that "at no period, not even in *Mardi*, does it seem right to think of him as other than a critic of transcendentalism."[18]

Melville's quarrel with Transcendentalism seems to have grown largely from his inability to accept what he regarded as its bland optimism and its failure to conceive of evil as a positive force operative in a mindless universe. This note is struck in the opening chapter of *Moby-Dick*, in which Melville's spokesman, Ishmael, says, "Not ignoring what is good, I am quick to perceive a horror" and indicates his readiness to accept it as one of "the inmates of the place one lodges in." Furthermore, if, as the disciples of the Newness insisted, the will was free, Melville must insist that it was as free to do evil as to do good. Thus Ahab, who will "strike the sun if it insulted me. . . . Who's over me? Truth hath no confines." As Matthiessen has seen, Melville "created in Ahab's tragedy a fearful symbol of the self-enclosed individualism that, carried to its furthest extreme, brings disaster both upon itself and upon the group of which it is part."[19]

In that most bitter of Melville's books, *Pierre,* he surrounds Pierre in New York with a group of new-light Apostles who attempt to ameliorate his sufferings by suggesting in the vein of the Transcendental doctrine of Compensation that misery does not truly exist. Indeed Schneider goes so far as to say that "any attempt to identify transcendental principles with 'civilized' standards seemed to Melville diabolical. He had only contempt for thinkers like Emerson, who, he said, are 'cracked right across the brow.'. . ."[20] And surely the pen portraits of Plotinus Plinlimmon in *Pierre* and the philosopher-mystic in *The Confidence Man* bear a suspicious likeness to Emerson, as one inclined to caricature might have viewed "the wisest American."

Despite the severity of some of the criticism of Transcendentalism, as we shall observe in our next chapter, even many of its critics were considerably influenced by some of the ideas of the Movement. Poe, Hawthorne, and Melville were among them.

CHAPTER 10

Influences of Transcendentalism on American Life and Literature

NO one can say with assurance just when the Transcendental Movement, that began with the publication of Emerson's *Nature* and the founding of the Transcendental Club in 1836, reached its high-water mark and started to ebb. The years of greatest excitement appear, however, to extend from 1836 through about 1843. By the latter date the meetings of the Club had ceased, Brook Farm came to the end of its purely Transcendental phase and began its transition to Fourierist Phalanx, Alcott's Fruitlands began and ended, *The Dial* was straining to continue publication, Brownson was on the verge of his conversion to Roman Catholicism, and other advocates of the movement were increasingly devoting themselves to particular reform causes such as Abolition and women's rights or to their own private ends. We may recall that Theodore Parker strove to rekindle the old enthusiasm in 1853 by calling for renewed meetings of the Transcendental Club but that his call went unanswered.

Although the movement as such may have been of relatively short duration, its influence has continued to be felt in a variety of ways down to the present day. And two of its three greatest literary statements—*Walden* and *Leaves of Grass*—were published after the crest, in 1854 and 1855 respectively.

In the present chapter we shall examine first the influence of Transcendentalism as it affected certain aspects of American civilization in the second half of the nineteenth century and into the twentieth century. Then we shall look at its impact on particular American writers of distinction other than such widely recognized Transcendentalists as Emerson, Thoreau, and Whitman. For, as Simon and Parsons have remarked, "A movement

[Transcendental Movement] that resisted definition at the start has been pervasive enough to have influenced subsequent movements as disjunct as Naturalism and Neo-Humanism and to have affected writers as opposed in their loyalties as Irving Babbitt and Eugene O'Neill."[1]

There was, of course, a body of men who quite consciously thought of themselves as Transcendentalists and who tried to carry on the ideals and ideas of the earlier generation into post Civil War America. Samuel Johnson, John Weiss, Samuel Longfellow, Thomas Wentworth Higginson, David A. Wasson, Moncure Conway, Octavius B. Frothingham—these were among the best known. Worthy as they were, they seemed to lack the spark of those who had generated the movement. And some of the ancient sages lingered on, creating in Concord itself what Brooks has referred to as an "afterglow of Transcendentalism."[2] For example, there was the Concord School of Philosophy that Alcott and William T. Harris of the St. Louis Hegelians founded in 1879 to combat the materialistic trend of scientific thinking. For nine summers young students, mostly from the West, where Alcott had indefatigably lectured, flocked there to take the courses on Emerson, Plato, Dante, Goethe, or Oriental religions, and to listen to William James lecture on psychology or Harrison Blake read from his friend Thoreau's unpublished journals.[3]

Of far wider-ranging importance, however, was the gathering movement of mind cure through the power of positive thinking that resulted in such phenomena as New Thought and Christian Science. Phineas Parkhurst Quimby pioneered both in his search for a way to cure the sick. Born a year before Emerson, he came to manhood as the Transcendental Movement was just beginning to stir. No intellectual, he was nonetheless plainly touched by the basic idea of the movement, for he came to consider himself as an agent "revealing that the power of curing was the divine wisdom in all of us accessible through intuition."[4]

Quimby died in 1866, and following his death a split in the religious faith-healing movement occurred, with Mary Baker Eddy establishing the Christian Science Church and Warren F. Evans, a Swedenborgian minister, combining New Thought with the Hegelian idea that thought is the greatest creative force in the world.[5]

Huber distinguishes Christian Science from New Thought thus:

Christian Science is closely organized and rigidly centralized with a u-
nified doctrine and an absolute discipline over its practitioners. In matters
of faith, the absolute idealism of Christian Science denies the existence
of matter and the reality of suffering. The New Thought movement consists of independent sects loosely organized . . . and centering authority
in no book or person . . . it does not deny the existence of sickness, sin
and poverty, but asserts that these evils can be overcome by right
thinking.[6]

Donald Meyer opines that "mind cure conventionalized lyric
transcendentalism into a prosy pragmatism. . ."[7] Indeed, the
mind cure theologists made the inevitable connection with Emerson and the Transcendentalists.[8] With no real philosophers
among them, they had a tendency to plunder Emerson's works in
particular for those ideas that fitted nicely into their theories of
health, wealth, and power through mind, which is God. It was
doubtless the metaphysics of practical idealism that they taught
which fascinated William James, who saw that "the heart of mind
cure was its psychology, and the heart of that psychology was its
displacement of consciousness. Consciousness could not be
trusted."[9] In developing his theory of the subconscious and its
importance to human behavior, James seems to have credited it
with almost magical powers that needed only to be obeyed. As
Meyer remarks, "Much of his description of the subconscious
amounted to no more than a new label for the famous faculty of
transcendental reason or intuition celebrated in New England
sixty years earlier."[10] Meyer goes on to point out that in its
poetic-philosophic form the transcendental idea of intuition was
not acceptable to scientific psychologists, but that essentially the
same idea wearing the cloak of the "subconscious" was acceptable
because it appeared to be more open to study and explanation.
Nonetheless it was characterized by traits associated with the religious faculty, traits that facilitated the individual's spiritual experience most directly in its best and fullest form.[11]

The connection between Emerson's doctrines and the new
mind-cure religion quite plainly existed, even though it might be
somewhat tenuous. After all, Transcendental doctrine seemed to
deny the reality of matter and stressed the power of mind. And
Emerson had contended that sickness should not be named; for it
was a kind of evil which, being negative, could scarcely be said to
exist.[12] Robert Peel has shown the warm reception accorded

Mary Baker Glover Eddy's *Science and Health* in 1876 on its publication,[13] and surely her refusal to accept disease, pain, old age, and death as realities, because such notions are applicable to matter rather than to spirit, which is the true reality, suggest at least a dim reflection of Emersonian attitudes. That Mrs. Eddy's ideas attracted at least some of the Transcendentalists is shown, for example, by Alcott's active interest in her book, which led him to visit her classes in Lynn and lecture to them.[14] What made her new church particularly attractive to many members of the upper middle class was its tight discipline and its apparent rejection of New Thought's religious pragmatism that "guaranteed sick people health, poor people riches, and troubled people happiness."[15] Unlike New Thought it did not embrace the "success" idea.[16]

It is, of course, not only through religious or mental healing movements that American Transcendentalism has continued to exert an influence in the United States, and in other parts of the world as well. Carpenter, for example, has suggested that its influence in India, through Gandhi's extensive reading of Emerson and Thoreau, is considerable. He has also produced evidence of the practical impact of their thought on the leaders of modern India.[17] And Lyons has advanced the view that the Austrian educator and social philosopher Rudolf Steiner and his Waldorf Schools—of which there are eight in the United States and some eighty in seventeen countries—show an affinity with Alcott's experiments in education and also with the basic ideals of Transcendentalism. For Steiner's Anthroposophy was to be "a way of knowledge that would lead the spiritual in man to the spiritual in the universe."[18]

In the United States the New Humanism of the scholars Irving Babbitt and Paul Elmer More was at least partly traceable to the Transcendental influence. Babbitt's studies of Indian philosophy would have been unlikely without the initial inspiration of the Orientalism of the American Transcendentalists, including Emerson, of whom Babbitt was, according to René Wellek, at times a conscious disciple.[19] He disapproved, however, of Emerson's undue optimism and of the romantic enterprise of reconciling man and nature.[20] Nevertheless he felt the need of the "pure supernatural light" that he saw in Transcendentalism.[21]

In the first half of the present century the influence of Transcendentalism in America, with the exception of its effect on a number of writers whom we shall discuss shortly, appeared largely dissipated. With the almost total triumph of materialism in an increasingly mechanized society, the Transcendental ideals seemed to have no place. The cumulative experience of two World Wars, a Great Depression, a Korean war and a Southeast Asian war has, however, brought about a resurgence of those ideals from about 1950 to the present. In the 50s the emergence of the "Beat" protest was a first straw in the wind. With its rebellion against the tyranny of possessions, of highly organized social structure, of the encroachments of the police state mentality, it was, despite the leftist radicalism of many of its members, an essentially apolitical movement, "a last-ditch stand for individualism and against conformity."[22]

By the 1960s and early 1970s many young Americans whom Huber calls the New Romantics were engaged in a spontaneous movement of dissent from the success creed that had motivated their parents. Rebelling against the work ethic that had led the Puritans to embrace work rather than leisure in the name of God's will and that had led their parents to prefer work over leisure in behalf of the God of national security proclaimed by their government, they "turned their backs," in Huber's words, "on the American goals of mobility and crass achievement."[23] Clad in the unisex uniform of blue jeans, they wore their hair long and smoked their marijuana joints short. Again to quote Huber, they "were social evolutionists engaged in a peaceful, non-political protest against the competitive ethic of success. Dropouts from the traditional values of steady work, competition, and status-seeking (with its anxieties), they proclaimed a life of meditation, cooperation, sensory gratification, and pleasure now."[24]

Some of them involved themselves in "transcendental meditation" as taught by gurus oriental and occidental; many went to live in communes where cooperation and doing one's own thing went hand in hand; and all were concerned about what they viewed as the rapidly deteriorating quality of life in America. In these ways they were logical descendants of the Transcendentalists; however, they seemed largely to lack the urge to reform that was so much a part of the earlier movement. And they were, by and large, far less philosophically or intellectually inclined. But the Thoreauvian advice to simplify one's life and to live in harmony with nature rather than as nature's adversary appeared to be at the root of their concept.

Turning now to the influence of Transcendentalism on American writers, we shall observe that it has been fairly constant since the early days of the movement. Of course, it is more difficult to discern in some than in others, but it would be scarcely an exaggeration to say that few of our foremost literary figures have been untouched by it.

In the preceding chapter attention was paid to the criticism of Transcendentalism by Poe, Hawthorne, and Melville at a time when the movement was at or near its peak. Despite the predominantly adverse attitude that we examined there, each one of them may also be seen as reflective in one way or another of at least certain aspects of the Transcendentalist rationale.

Poe, for example, has been viewed by more than one astute critic as adopting the Transcendentalist position particularly in his *Eureka*, where he bridges the gap between truth and poetry (beauty) he had so frequently insisted on. Arnold Smithline sees him as advocating in this poem the intuitive over the rational approach:

Thus we see that Poe's ideas in *Eureka* are very close indeed to Transcendentalism. . . . In his assertion of the unity of man and the cosmos, and of reliance upon intuition as the best means of realizing that ultimate Truth, Poe is following the main tenets of the Transcendentalists. His final vision is not a descent into the maelstrom of nothingness but a positive assertion of man's divinity.[25]

Conner agrees that *Eureka* has a transcendental conclusion although he does not see the entire work in that light. For Conner, Poe pushed his mechanistic attitude "to the conclusion that God is all, and in so doing pushed himself at least part way into the camp of the scorned transcendentalists."[26] In like manner Conner views Longfellow as distrustful of all transcendentalism but accepting and molding some transcendental doctrines to his conservative Unitarian Christianity.[27]

Marjorie Elder has devoted an entire volume to establishing with voluminous documentation Hawthorne's debt to the Transcendentalists' aesthetic theories, which she also sees as influencing many other critics of Transcendentalism, such as Longfellow, Lowell, Holmes, and Melville. Tellingly, she quotes Longfellow:

"The highest exercise of imagination is not to devise what has no existence, but rather to perceive what really exists, though unseen by the outward eye,—not creation, but insight."[28] Here he is surely at one with Emerson.

Hawthorne speaks specifically in such works as "The Hall of Fantasy," "The Old Manse," and the preface to "Rappaccini's Daughter" of the influence of the Transcendentalist aesthetic theories as carefully formulated and published by Emerson. Indeed Elder believes that "Hawthorne, like Emerson, saw Reality shadowed in the Actual; the Perfect in the Imperfect—in Nature and Man. Hawthorne's Artist, like Emerson's, was the last best touch of the Creator, enabled by Faith, Intuition, the pursuit of Beauty and by Nature's revelations to him to create an image of the Ideal."[29] In fact she sees Hawthorne as carrying out the Transcendentalist aesthetic by mingling the Actual and the Imaginative throughout his tales. He is, she holds, using Transcendental symbolism by doing so in his assertion of Truth as well as by arranging scenes in correspondence with Nature.[30] In like manner, she believes that "Melville's symbolic method of striking through the mask was thoroughly Transcendental."[31]

That Melville was opposed to Emersonian Transcendentalism as a philosophy we have already remarked, but that there are echoes of that philosophy too numerous to mention in such books as *Mardi* and *Moby-Dick* the most casual reader may discern. Indeed in his last work, *Billy Budd*, written long after the movement was at its height, Melville seems to accept an essential tenet of the Transcendentalists, and most certainly of Emerson, namely, that society everywhere is conspiring against the manhood of its members. For Captain Vere, who condemns the Christ-like Billy, is the very symbol of that conformity that makes of the human being not a man but a uniformed robot. Vere's tragedy is that he is sensitive enough to know it.

Even the "Genteel Poets" of the latter part of the nineteenth century were touched by the Transcendental concepts. As Conner has shown, the broker-poet E.C. Stedman in *Nature and Elements* and in such a poem as "Fin de Siècle" displays his interpretation of the divine immanence as the private soul universalized, a distinctly Transcendental concept.[32] And Richard Watson Gilder thought of the material universe after the Transcendental fashion as simply an expression or manifestation of God!

"His God both was and was not the universe, was transcendent as well as immanent."[33]

As for the greatest American poet of the latter half of the nineteenth century other than Whitman, Emily Dickinson, there is ample evidence that she absorbed Transcendental ideas as well as the Emersonian spirit and thus became, in the words of Clark Griffith, a "post-Emersonian, or, still more accurately perhaps, a sort of Emersonian-in-reverse."[34]

Such poems as 632, "The Brain is Wider than the Sky," composed perhaps in 1862, and 1510, "How happy is the little Stone," written perhaps in 1881, suggest quite clearly the Transcendental inspiration.[35] The first, stating the unlimited measurements of the human mind—"wider than the sky," "deeper than the sea," and "just the weight of God"—implies the divinity of man and his identification with the universal being, a fundamental Transcendental tenet. And the second, about the happy little stone "That rambles in the Road alone," not concerned with fashioning a career or with fearsome exigencies, created by universal force to be "independent as the Sun," and "Fulfilling absolute Decree in casual simplicity" reflects the Transcendental ideals of individual freedom, closeness to nature, simplicity in living, and the divinely ordered universe.

Still other poems with a distinct Transcendental thrust are 501, "This World is not Conclusion"; 668, " 'Nature' is what we see"; 669, "No Romance sold unto"; 1176, "We never know how high we are"; 1354, "The Heart is the Capital of the Mind"; and 1355, "The Mind lives on the Heart."

As Cambon has pointed out, Dickinson was, however, ambivalent in her transcendentalism, apparently feeling at times, as in 280, that she has no over-soul to rely on in her existential plight.[36] The poem describes the funeral in her brain as she realizes her desperate isolation as an earthbound member of the human race. "And then a Plank in Reason [the Transcendentalist intuitive wisdom], broke, she says, letting her drop terrifyingly from world to world until, ambiguously, she "Finished knowing—then—" as the poem ends.

Even such a relatively sophisticated literary practitioner as William Dean Howells, author of almost forty novels, esteemed critic, and editor of such influential journals as *The Atlantic Monthly* and *Harpers*, is seen to have a kinship with the New England

Transcendentalists because of his Swedenborgian background, a kinship most marked during his period of Utopian social reform.[37] It may be discerned in such novels as *The World of Chance* (1893) in which we meet an old socialist, David Hughes, who had once been a member of the Brook Farm community and who serves as Howells's spokesman in suggesting that society is not to be reformed by individuals who are simply interested in improving themselves, but by those who will work together to reconstruct its institutions. *A Traveller from Altruria* (1894) and its sequel, *Through the Eye of the Needle* (1907), present Howells's social idealism by contrasting the growing inequities of American life and its laissez-faire economic system to his utopian view that reiterates the Transcendental vision of the potential value of each man and the perfectibility of human society.

The Transcendental influence extends into the present century in the thought of such eminent poets as Frost and Stevens, such a dramatist as O'Neill, and such voices of the "Beat Generation" as those of Allen Ginsberg and Gary Snyder.

That Robert Frost had a lifelong interest in Emerson is attested not only by much of his poetry but also by his biographer, Lawrance Thompson. William Chamberlain in his essay "The Emersonianism of Robert Frost"[38] sees it as "central to an understanding of the core of Frost's philosophy of poetry, the concept of a 'momentary stay against confusion.'" Chamberlain presents such poems as "West-Running Brook" and "Directive" as prime evidence. The former poem contains a conversation between husband and wife about the brook that runs west contrary to all the other country brooks that run east to reach the ocean. The husband explains toward the end of the poem:

> It is this backward motion toward the source,
> Against the stream, that most we see ourselves in,
> the tribute of the current to the source.
> It is from this in nature we are from.
> It is most us.

This seeming identification of the human being's origin with a common natural source, a universal being, is thoroughly transcendental as is the somewhat more obscure admonition in "Directive" in which the poet directs us back to a hidden brook that once provided water for a farm house long gone and tells us to "drink and be whole again beyond confusion." Nor should we overlook the thoroughly Transcendental rejection of thoughtless adherence to tradition that forms the basis of one of Frost's best-known poems, "Mending Wall."

Frost, brought up in a Swedenborgian household, was a self-proclaimed mystic who believed in symbols and who, through their use, suggests again and again in his poems the Emersonian, Thoreauvian requirement that man must establish a primary contact with nature in order to give any meaning to his life. It is scarcely surprising, then, to find him listing Emerson's *Essays* and *Poems* and Thoreau's *Walden* among the ten books he believed should be in every public library.[39]

Although a transcendental influence may seem far from surprising in a "country" poet like Frost, its presence in a poet so urbane and sophisticated as Wallace Stevens may be unexpected. But, as Nina Baym has fully demonstrated, it is there in full measure. Contrary to the frequently expressed idea that Stevens rejected Transcendentalism, she finds that "line by line. . .his kinship manifests itself."[40] Noting that the Transcendentalists, despite their insistence on a universal mind, recognized that each human being continued to apprehend, conceive, and perceive through his own mind, she observes that Stevens, however he may insist "that each man's perception is discrete and cannot be related back to an overarching unity, believes very strongly that the experience of any one mind is common to all minds." Thus she finds in Stevens' poetry a modern version of Transcendentalism.[41]

Baym further notes that Stevens' poetry may be interpreted as a modern attempt to articulate the Transcendental moment of ecstasy proclaimed so strikingly by Emerson. She finds, however, that it is Thoreau more than Emerson or any other Transcendentalist that Stevens resembles. The reason is their sharing of "an overwhelming love for landscape, which leads them both to dedicate themselves to nature in poetry with the same sort of novitiate intensity."[42] Beyond sharing this love of nature, she sees Thoreau and Stevens formulating their principal emotions —joy and despair—in much the same way. Both are also seen as preoccupied with change as an immutable fact of the universe (perhaps the Platonic doctrine of flux?). "From 'Sunday Morning' on through all his works," she says, "Stevens asserted that al-

though we *think* we love stability, in fact everything in the world
that we love, and even love itself, originates from change. 'Death
is the mother of beauty'. . . *Walden,* as much as 'Sunday Morning,' is an attempt to show the world enduring through
change. . . ."[43]

Many examples can be found among Stevens' poems to illustrate his transcendental point of view. For example, in "The
Planet on the Table" he writes of the poet:

> His self and the sun were one
> And his poems, although makings of his self,
> Were no less makings of the sun.

Here we see the identification of the self with divinity (the Sun)
and the Emersonian notion of poetry all existing in nature before
time was.

In what is perhaps Stevens' most famous poem, "Sunday Morning," we observe the modern woman unable to devote herself to
the conventional worship of dead gods. The poet asks

> Why should she give her bounty to the dead?
> What is divinity if it can come
> Only in silent shadows and in dreams?
> Shall she not find in comforts of the sun,
> In pungent fruit and bright, green wings, or else
> In any balm or beauty of the earth,
> Things to be cherished like the thought of heaven?
> Divinity must live within herself. . .

Here Stevens has brilliantly encapsulated three main tenets of
Transcendentalist doctrine: that the God of the established
churches is a dead, historical God who can no longer inspire
faith; that religious ecstasy is to be found through contact with
nature; and that the living God can be found only within the self.
The poem further emphasizes Stevens' rejection of the sterile,
changeless, conventionalized Heaven in favor of the ever-
changing beauties of the earthly here and now.

Or again, in such a poem as "Final Soliloquy of the Interior
Paramour" we see the suggestion of the individual mind being
one with a central mind (like the Transcendental over-soul) as
part of a dimly divined order that we know through feeling or intuition. The final three stanzas say it best:

Here, now, we forget each other and ourselves,
We feel the obscurity of an order, a whole,
A knowledge, that which arranged the rendezvous.

Within its vital boundary, in the mind.
We say God and the imagination are one. . .
How high that highest candle lights the dark.

Out of this same light, out of the central mind,
We make a dwelling in the evening air,
In which being there together is enough.

In American drama Eugene O'Neill, currently undergoing a great revival of interest, is the only significant playwright to have reflected something of the Transcendental attitude. As he once wrote to the drama critic George Jean Nathan, "The playwright of today must dig at the roots of the sickness of today as he feels it—the death of the old God and the failure of science and materialism to give any satisfactory new one for the surviving primitive, religious instinct to find a meaning for life in, and to comfort its fears of death with."[44] This is indeed what the Transcendentalists of a hundred years before had felt that they must do. The difference between them and an O'Neill lies in their belief that they had discovered a cure for the pervasive sickness.

O'Neill is seen by Carpenter as ambivalent in his feelings toward the Transcendentalists. Like him they had been "rebels against the materialism of their times, but their idealism had also been the product of a Yankee and Puritan society,"[45] a society that O'Neill scorned for its narrow hypocrisies (in, e.g., *Beyond the Horizon* and *Desire Under the Elms*). Emerson and Thoreau, says Carpenter, never scorned material things but sought to ameliorate the actual situation, and appealed to the future. O'Neill, on the other hand, had no belief in the future or any hope for it. Tragedy he considered essential to the nature of things. Thus, in a sense, Carpenter finds him even more transcendental than the optimistic Emerson.[46]

"Historic Transcendentalism," Carpenter comments, "has, in fact, divided into two streams. The first has become active, scientific, and pragmatic. The second has become passive, mystical, and psychological. Emerson's thought flowed largely in the first stream, toward modern pragmatism. O'Neill's thought tended towards modern, nonrational psychology."[47] Thus O'Neill's marked interest in, and use of, Freudian probings into the less accessible reaches of the human psyche as a means of comprehending the mysterious behavior of his fellow travelers on the planet Earth.

Turning to the more immediate scene, we find such poets as Allen Ginsberg and Gary Snyder carrying on, each in his own way, the tradition of Whitman and Thoreau. Ginsberg quite plainly accepts Whitman's concept of the poet as teacher, prophet, and seer. And he writes his verse in the same free and irregular lines, with a vocabulary geared to the colloquial diction of his own time and place. Although his view of America lacks the optimistic note of the author of *Leaves of Grass*, he shares the Transcendental will to protest against an established majority that is leveling the nation into a deadly mediocrity.

As Ginsberg was the Beat Generation's approximation of Whitman, so has Snyder been its latter-day version of Thoreau. Intensely interested, as was Thoreau, in the literature and philosophy of the Orient, he learned Chinese and Japanese and even lived for a time in a Buddhist monastery. And like Thoreau he has been intensely concerned with the physical environment of America. Nor can the preoccupation in his verse with the need to be free and on the move be overlooked, so much is it in the tradition of Thoreau.

In conclusion, it is impossible not to agree with Edwin Gittleman's view that "contrary to the commonplace assertion that the Civil War effectively destroyed the transcendental ambiance in America, the magical Circle of Concord has never really been broken. Rather, it has been expanded to where now it seems to touch (if not embrace) a perplexing demi-world consisting of Allen Ginsberg, the Beatles, S.D.S., Abbie Hoffman, sexual freedoms, Black Power, lysergic acid diethylamide, and miscellaneous esoterica and erotica."[48] Even though Gay Wilson Allen may be right in remarking that the main difficulty for one today trying to teach the Transcendentalists is that their goal of a deeper spiritual life has become "an almost meaningless abstraction," his further observation that they were trying to find a more satisfying life here and now on this lovely earth[49] is perhaps equally true of many of those mentioned in Gittleman's catalogue of the contemporary underground that cannot accept the values of the American establishment.

To close this book on American Transcendentalism without giving the last word to its foremost spokesman, Ralph Waldo Emerson, would seem almost an act of heresy. In his journal for 1841 he said of it, "That it has a necessary place in history is a fact not to be overlooked, not possibly to be prevented, and however discredited to the heedless & to the moderate & conservative persons by the foibles or inadequacy of those who partake the movement yet is it the pledge & the herald of all that is dear to the human heart, grand & inspiring to human faith."[50]

Notes and References

Chapter One

1. Octavius B. Frothingham, *Transcendentalism in New England* (New York, 1959), p. xxv. First published in 1876.
2. *The Letters of Ralph Waldo Emerson*, ed. Ralph L. Rusk (New York, 1939), II, 266.
3. Frothingham, p. 136.
4. *Ibid.*, p. 138.
5. Frederic I. Carpenter, *Emerson Handbook* (New York, 1953), pp. 128–29.
6. Harold Clarke Goddard, *Studies in New England Transcendentalism* (New York, 1908), p. 196.
7. Walter L. Leighton, *French Philosophers and New England Transcendentalism* (Charlottesville, Va., 1908), p. 5.
8. Kenneth Walter Cameron, *Young Emerson's Transcendental Vision; an exposition of his world view with an analysis of the structure, backgrounds, and meaning of Nature (1836)* (Hartford, 1971), p. 7.
9. Ralph Waldo Emerson, *The Journals and Miscellaneous Notebooks* (Cambridge, Mass., 1964), VIII, 313.
10. William R. Hutchison, *The Transcendental Ministers; Church Reform in the New England Renaissance* (Hamden, Conn., 1972), p. 23.
11. *Ibid.*
12. Leonora Cranch Scott, *The Life and Letters of Christopher Pearse Cranch* (Boston and New York, 1917), p. 51.

Chapter Two

1. Hutchison, *The Transcendental Ministers*, p. 3.
2. Goddard, *Studies in New England Transcendentalism*, p. 185.
3. Hutchison, p. 4.
4. *Ibid.*, p. 5.
5. Stephen E. Whicher, *Freedom and Fate; An Inner Life of Ralph Waldo Emerson* (Philadelphia, 1953), p. 7.
6. Goddard, pp. 185–86.
7. *Ibid.*, p. 188.

8. Merle Curti, *The Growth of American Thought,* 2nd ed. *(New York, 1951)*, p. 304.
9. Hutchison, p. 24.
10. Frothingham, *Transcendentalism in New England*, p. 21.
11. *Ibid.*, p. 46.
12. Curti, p. 304.
13. "The Minor Transcendentalists and German Philosophy," *New England Quarterly* XV (1942), 652–80.
14. Tony Tanner, *The Reign of Wonder; Naivety and Reality in American Literature* (New York, 1967), p. 9.
15. *Ibid.*, p. 5.
16. Arthur E. Christy, *The Orient in American Transcendentalism: A Study of Emerson, Thoreau, and Alcott* (New York, 1932), pp. 182–83.
17. *Ibid.*, p. 188.
18. Frederic I. Carpenter, *Emerson and Asia* (Cambridge, Mass., 1930), pp. 250–51.
19. *Ibid.*, p. 26.
20. Wilcomb E. Washburn, "The Orient in Mid-Nineteenth Century American Literature," *The Southwestern Journal* V, no. i (1949–50), 74.
21. Washburn, "The Oriental 'Roots' of American Transcendentalism," *The Southwestern Journal* IV, no. iv (1949), 141.
22. *Ibid.*, pp. 152–53.
23. *The Selected Writings of Ralph Waldo Emerson*, ed. Brooks Atkinson (New York, 1950), p. 49.
24. Whicher, p. 151.
25. Van Wyck Brooks, *The Flowering of New England* (New York, 1936), p. 187.

Chapter Three

1. Emerson, *Journals,* V, entry of Sept. 20, 1836, pp. 194–95.
2. Odell Shepard, *Pedlar's Progress: The Life of Bronson Alcott* (Boston, 1937), pp. 248–49.
3. Ralph L. Rusk, *The Life of Ralph Waldo Emerson* (New York, 1949), p. 244.
4. Emerson, *Journals,* V, 195.
5. Rusk, p. 243.
6. *Ibid.*, p. 256.
7. No truly authoritative list of the membership exists, if one was ever kept.
8. Lindsay Swift, *Brook Farm: Its Members, Scholars, and Visitors* (New York and London, 1900), p. 9.

9. Emerson, *Selected Writings,* p. 52.
10. Shepard, p. 254.
11. Arthur A. Ekirch, *The Idea of Progress in America, 1815–1860* (New York, 1944), p. 51.
12. *Ibid.,* p. 158.
13. Curti, *Growth of American Thought,* p. 304.
14. Shepard, p. 268.
15. Ekirch, p. 155.
16. Emerson, *Journals,* VIII, 382.
17. As reprinted in *Autobiography of Brook Farm,* ed. Henry W. Sams (Englewood Cliffs, N.J., 1958), p. 45.
18. *Ibid.,* pp. 46–47.
19. Brooks, *Flowering of New England,* p. 251.
20. Emerson, "Historic Notes of Life and Letters in New England," in *Ralph Waldo Emerson, Selected Prose and Poetry,* 2nd ed., ed. Reginald L. Cook (New York, 1969), p. 280.
21. Journal entry for October 17, 1840, as reprinted in Sams, pp. 4–5.
22. Sams, p. 7.
23. *Ibid.,* pp. 10–11.
24. Henry David Thoreau, *Journal,* ed. Bradford Torrey and Francis H. Allen (Boston, 1906), I, 227.
25. *The Heart of Hawthorne's Journals,* ed. Newton Arvin (Boston and New York, 1929), p. 75.
26. As quoted in Swift, p. 14.
27. Swift, p. 69.
28. *Ibid.,* p. 14.
29. *Ibid.,* pp. 35–36.
30. Sams, p. 201.
31. Emerson, "Historic Notes" in Cook, p. 284.
32. Clara Endicott Sears, *Bronson Alcott's Fruitlands* (Boston and New York, 1915), p. 12.
33. From *Silver Pitchers* (1876), reprinted in *The Transcendentalist Revolt Against Materialism,* ed. George F. Whicher (Boston, 1949), p. 103.
34. Emerson, *Journals,* VIII, 218.
35. Clarence L. F. Gohdes, *The Periodicals of American Transcendentalism* (Durham, N.C., 1931), p. 37.
36. Paul R. Anderson, *Platonism in the Midwest* (New York and London, 1963), p. 16.
37. Henry A. Pochmann, *New England Transcendentalism and St. Louis Hegelianism* (Philadelphia, 1948).
38. Frances B. Harmon, *The Social Philosophy of the St. Louis Hegelians* (New York, 1943), p. 1.
39. *Ibid.*

40. *Ibid.*, pp. 2–4.
41. *Ibid.*, p. 101.

Chapter Four

1. Rusk, *Life of Emerson*, p. 275.
2. Frothingham, *Transcendentalism in New England*, p. 133.
3. *Ibid.*
4. *The Transcendentalists, An Anthology*, ed. Perry Miller (Cambridge, Mass., 1950), p. 248.
5. "The Critical Stance of *The Dial*," in *The Minor and Later Transcendentalists, A Symposium*, ed. Edwin Gittleman (Hartford, 1969), p. 26.
6. Gohdes, *Periodicals of American Transcendentalism*, p. 37.
7. Paul O. Williams in his unpublished University of Pennsylvania dissertation, *The Transcendental Movement in American Poetry* (Philadelphia, 1962), p. 459, concurs in this evaluation, partly on the ground that they were mystics, whereas poets like Cranch and Ellery Channing were not.
8. Gohdes, p. 80.
9. *The Correspondence of Emerson and Carlyle*, ed. Joseph Slater (New York, 1964), pp. 328–29.
10. Miller, p. 372.
11. As reprinted in Miller, p. 374.
12. *Ibid.*
13. Emerson, *Selected Writings*, pp. 322–23.
14. Miller, p. 411.
15. *Ibid.*, p. 412.
16. *Ibid.*, p. 310.
17. Marjorie J. Elder, *Nathaniel Hawthorne, Transcendental Symbolist* (Athens, Ohio, 1969), p. 37.
18. *The Portable Thoreau*, ed. Carl Bode (New York, 1947), p. 193.
19. Norman Foerster, "Emerson on the Organic Principle in Art" as reprinted in *Emerson*, ed. Milton R. Konvitz and Stephen E. Whicher (Englewood Cliffs, N.J., 1962), p. 114.
20. Elder, p. 15.
21. John Q. Anderson, *The Liberating Gods; Emerson on Poets and Poetry* (Coral Gables, Fla., 1971), p. 94.

Chapter Five

1. Emerson, *Letters*, III, 18.
2. Emerson, *Selected Writings*, p. 92.
3. Sherman Paul, *Emerson's Angle of Vision* (Cambridge, Mass., 1952), p. 7.

4. Emerson, *Journals*, I, 141–43.
5. Paul, p. 13.
6. *Ibid.*, p. 10.
7. Miller, *The Transcendentalists*, p. 250.
8. Shepard, *Pedlar's Progress*, p. 259.
9. Kenneth Burke, "I, Eye, Ay—Emerson's Early Essay 'Nature': Thoughts on the Machinery of Transcendence," in *Transcendentalism and Its Legacy*, ed. Myron Simon and Thornton H. Parsons (Ann Arbor, 1966), p. 9.
10. Emerson, *Selected Writings*, p. 6.
11. *Ibid.*
12. *Ibid.*, p. 7.
13. *Ibid.*, p. 9.
14. *Ibid.*, p. 13.
15. *Ibid.*, p. 17.
16. *Ibid.*, p. 24.
17. S. Whicher, *Freedom and Fate*, pp. 53–54
18. Emerson, *Selected Writings*, p. 33.
19. *Ibid.*, p. 34.
20. *Ibid.*, p. 36.
21. *Ibid.*, pp. 37–38.
22. Whether the poet was Bronson Alcott or Emerson himself is a matter of some dispute among scholars of the subject.
23. Emerson, *Selected Writings*, p. 42.
24. Kenneth Walter Cameron, *Emerson the Essayist*, 2 vols. (Raleigh, N.C., 1945), I, 361.
25. Emerson, *Selected Writings*, p. 62.
26. *Ibid.*, p. 73.
27. *Ibid.*, p. 79.
28. *Ibid.*, p. 81.
29. S. Whicher, p. 43.
30. *Ibid.*, pp. 40–42.
31. Rusk, *Life of Emerson*, p. 279.
32. Emerson, *Journals*, IV, 68.
33. Emerson, *Selected Writings*, p. 148.
34. *Ibid.*, p. 156.
35. *Ibid.*, p. 163.
36. *Ibid.*, p. 168.
37. Rusk, p. 283.
38. S. Whicher, p. 69.
39. Emerson, *Selected Writings*, p. 262. Emerson gave his finest poetic expression to the idea in the last sentence of his poem "Brahma."
40. Jonathan Bishop, *Emerson on the Soul* (Cambridge, Mass., 1964), p. 32.

41. *Ibid.*, p. 165.
42. John S. Harrison, *The Teachers of Emerson* (New York, 1910), p. 8.
43. *Ibid.*, p. 144.
44. S. Whicher, pp. 20–21.
45. Emerson, *Journals*, V, 336.
46. Carpenter, *Emerson and Asia*, p. 77.
47. James E. Miller, Jr., "Uncharted Interiors: The American Romantics Revisited," *Emerson Society Quarterly*, XXXV (1964), 34–39.
48. Rusk, p. 283.
49. René Wellek, "Irving Babbitt, Paul More and Transcendentalism," in *Transcendentalism and Its Legacy*, p. 198.
50. Scott, *Life and Letters of C.P. Cranch*, p. 47.
51. Brooks, *Flowering of New England*, p. 203.
52. Arvin, *Heart of Hawthorne's Journals*, p. 99.
53. *The Letters of Herman Melville*, ed. Merrell R. Davis and William H. Gilman (New Haven, 1960).
54. Elder, *Hawthorne, Transcendental Symbolist*, p. 42.
55. Reprinted in Konvitz and Whicher, p. 31.
56. Floyd Stovall, *Eight American Authors* (New York, 1963), p. 62 ff.
57. Rusk, p. 95.
58. Emerson, *Selected Writings*, p. 69.
59. *Ibid.*, p. 185.
60. Newton Arvin, "The House of Pain," in Konvitz and Whicher, p. 54.
61. *Ibid.*, p. 53.
62. Emerson, *Selected Writings*, p. 845.
63. S. Whicher, pp. 77–78.
64. Emerson, *Selected Writings*, p. 451.
65. Emerson, *Journals*, IV, 84.
66. Emerson, *Selected Writings*, p. 513.
67. Emerson, *Journals*, IV, 278.
68. Goddard, *Studies in New England Transcendentalism*, pp. 185–86.
69. "The Influence of European Ideas in Nineteenth-Century America," *American Literature* VII (1935), 241, footnote 2.
70. Emerson, *Selected Writings*, p. 295.
71. Emerson R. Marks, "Victor Cousin and Emerson," in *Transcendentalism and Its Legacy*, p. 65.
72. Slater, *Correspondence of Emerson and Carlyle*, p. 7.
73. Philip L. Nicoloff, *Emerson on Race and History* (New York, 1961), p. 80.
74. Bishop, p. 144.
75. *Ibid.*, p. 205.

76. S. Whicher, pp. 124–25.
77. Paul, p. 224.

Chapter Six

1. Walter Harding, *The Days of Henry Thoreau* (New York, 1965), pp. 63–64.
2. Emerson, *Selected Writings*, p. 910.
3. *Ibid.*, p. 899.
4. *Ibid.*, p. 911.
5. *The Best of Thoreau's Journals*, ed. Carl Bode (Carbondale, Ill., 1967), p. 7.
6. Edward Mather, *Nathaniel Hawthorne* (New York, 1940), p. 334.
7. Arvin, *Heart of Hawthorne's Journals*, pp. 106–07.
8. Joel Porte, *Emerson and Thoreau: Transcendentalists in Conflict* (Middletown, Conn., 1965), pp. 192, 195–96.
9. *Correspondence of Henry David Thoreau*, ed. Walter Harding and Carl Bode (New York, 1958), p. 216.
10. Porte, p. 199.
11. *The Heart of Emerson's Journals*, ed. Bliss Perry (Boston and New York, 1926), p. 182.
12. Bode, *The Portable Thoreau*, p. 457.
13. Goddard, *Studies in New England Transcendentalism*, p. 193.
14. Bode, *Best of Thoreau's Journals*, p. 9.
15. Henry David Thoreau, *Journal* (New York, 1963), VII, 79–80.
16. Bode, *Portable Thoreau*, p. 343.
17. Harding, pp. 179–80.
18. *Ibid.*, pp. 187–88.
19. Bode, *Portable Thoreau*, p. 263.
20. *Ibid.*, p. 269.
21. *Ibid.*, p. 270.
22. *Ibid.*, p. 343.
23. *Ibid.*
24. *Ibid.*, p. 349.
25. *Ibid.*, pp. 349–50.
26. Harding, p. 334.
27. Bode, *Portable Thoreau*, pp. 562–63.
28. *Ibid.*, p. 113.
29. *Ibid.*, p. 122.
30. Harding, p. 418.
31. Bode, *Portable Thoreau*, pp. 678–79.
32. *Ibid.*, p. 632.
33. *Ibid.*, p. 634.

34. *Ibid.*, p. 636.
35. *Ibid.*
36. Emerson, *Journals*, V, 453.

Chapter Seven

1. In an anonymous review done for *Putnam's Magazine* in September, 1855.
2. *Song of Myself*, #21.
3. *Ibid.*, #24.
4. Conner, *Cosmic Optimism*, p. 101.
5. Gay Wilson Allen, *The Solitary Singer* (New York, 1955), p. 172.
6. *Song of Myself*, #1.
7. *Ibid.*, #51
8. Rufus M. Jones, *Studies in Mystical Religion* (London, 1909), p. 218.
9. Emerson, *Selected Writings*, p. 61.
10. Allen, p. 205.
11. *Leaves of Grass*, ed. Oscar Cargill (New York, 1950), p. 188.
12. *Ibid.*, p. 189.
13. Conner, p. 118.
14. See Chapter 3, p. 21.
15. *Song of Myself*, #23.

Chapter Eight

1. Shepard, *Pedlar's Progress*, p. 94.
2. *Ibid.*, p. 72.
3. *Ibid.*, p. 70.
4. Miller, *The Transcendentalists*, pp. 151–52.
5. Frothingham, *Transcendentalism in New England*, p. 267.
6. René Wellek, "The Minor Transcendentalists and German Philosophy," *New England Quarterly* XV, no. 4 (Dec., 1942), 652–80.
7. Frothingham, p. 259.
8. Miller, p. 241.
9. *Ibid.*, p. 243.
10. *Ibid.*, p. 242.
11. *The American Transcendentalists*, ed. Perry Miller (Garden City, N.Y., 1957), p. 39.
12. Frothingham, p. 358.
13. Ripley's congregation were devoted to him, but could not accept the views he expressed to them in a letter of October 1, 1840, in which he espoused the Transcendental philosophy, maintaining

that "the truth of religion does not depend on tradition, nor historical facts, but has an unerring witness in the soul." Thus on March 28, 1841, he preached a farewell discourse that deserves to rank in the forefront of heretical confessions. "One course only remained for me," he said, "—to give a full disclosure of all my heresies; to confess that I was a peace man, a temperance man, an abolitionist, a transcendentalist, a friend of radical reform in our social institutions; and if there be any other name that is contrary to sound doctrine, as now expounded by the masters in our Israel, to consent to bear whatever stigma might be attached to it. I was unwilling to sustain a false position for a moment." As quoted in Miller, *The Transcendentalists*, p. 259.

14. Miller, *The Transcendentalists*, pp. 469-70.
15. *Ibid.*, p. 70.
16. *Ibid.*, p. 69.
17. Ronald V. Wells, *Three Christian Transcendentalists* (New York, 1943), pp. 146–47.
18. *Ibid.*, pp. 147–48.
19. *Ibid.*, p. 150.
20. Miller, *The Transcendentalists*, pp. 47–48.
21. *Ibid.*, p. 226.
22. G. F. Whicher, *Transcendentalist Revolt*, p. 88.
23. Herbert W. Schneider, *A History of American Philosophy*, 2nd ed. (New York, 1963), pp. 229–30.
24. *Ibid.*, p. 224.
25. *Ibid.*, p. 227.
26. Miller, *The Transcendentalists*, p. 269.
27. Emerson, *Letters*, IV, 390, n.
28. Rusk, *Life of Emerson*, p. 404.
29. Miller, *The Transcendentalists*, pp. 485–86.
30. Henry Steele Commager, *Theodore Parker* (Boston, 1936), p. 196.
31. Miller, *The Transcendentalists*, p. 300.
32. *Ibid.*, p. 301.
33. William Irving Bartlett, *Jones Very, Emerson's Brave Saint* (Durham, N.C., 1942), p. 48.
34. *Ibid.*, p. 44.
35. Emerson, *Selected Writings*, p. 335.
36. Miller, *The Transcendentalists*, p. 356.
37. Elder, *Hawthorne, Transcendental Symbolist*, p. 6.
38. Miller, *The Transcendentalists*, p. 331.
39. Frothingham, p. 285.
40. *Ibid.*, p. 292.
41. Arvin, *Heart of Hawthorne's Journals*, pp. 270–71.
42. Frothingham, p. 299.

Chapter Nine

1. Emerson, *Journals*, VII, 388. Entry for July 31, 1840.
2. Hutchison, *Transcendental Ministers*, pp. 23–24.
3. Miller, *The Transcendentalists*, p. 159.
4. *Ibid.*
5. *Ibid.*, p. 193.
6. *Ibid.*, pp. 193–95.
7. Hutchison, p. 70.
8. Miller, *The Transcendentalists*, p. 210.
9. *Ibid.*, p. 213.
10. *Ibid.*, pp. 174–75.
11. Slater, *Correspondence of Emerson and Carlyle*, p. 277.
12. Joe Lee Davis, "Santayana as a Critic of Transcendentalism," in *Transcendentalism and Its Legacy*, p. 170.
13. *Ibid.*, pp. 160–61.
14. F. O. Matthiessen, *American Renaissance: Art and Expression in the Age of Emerson and Whitman* (New York, London and Toronto, 1941), p. 242.
15. Conner, *Cosmic Optimism*, p. 67.
16. *Selected Writings of Edgar Allan Poe*, ed. Edward H. Davidson (Boston, 1956), p. 468.
17. Matthiessen, p. 652.
18. *Ibid.*, p. 472, footnote.
19. *Ibid.*, p. 459.
20. Schneider, *American Philosophy*, p. 257.

Chapter Ten

1. Simon and Parsons, *Transcendentalism and Its Legacy*, Preface.
2. Van Wyck Brooks, *New England: Indian Summer* (New York and London, 1950), p. 340.
3. *Ibid.*, p. 342.
4. Richard M. Huber, *The American Idea of Success* (New York, 1971), p. 129.
5. *Ibid.*
6. *Ibid.*, p. 130.
7. Donald Meyer, *The Positive Thinkers* (Garden City, N.Y., 1966), p. 62.
8. Huber, p. 130.
9. Meyer, p. 65.
10. *Ibid.*, p. 68.
11. *Ibid.*
12. Brooks, *Indian Summer*, p. 343.

13. Robert Peel, *Christian Science. Its Encounter with American Culture* (New York, 1958).
14. Brooks, *Indian Summer*, p. 343.
15. Huber, p. 131.
16. *Ibid.*, p. 130.
17. Frederic I. Carpenter, "American Transcendentalism in India (1961)," *Emerson Society Quarterly*, XXXI (1963), 59–62.
18. Nathan Lyons, "Alcott and Rudolf Steiner: Educators of the Whole Man," in Gittleman, *The Minor and Later Transcendentalists*.
19. René Wellek, "Irving Babbitt, Paul More, and Transcendentalism," in *Transcendentalism and Its Legacy*, p. 192.
20. *Ibid.*, p. 195.
21. *Ibid.*, p. 202.
22. Bruce Cook, *The Beat Generation* (New York, 1971), p. 85.
23. Huber, p. 444.
24. *Ibid.*, p. 443.
25. Arnold Smithline, "*Eureka:* Poe As Transcendentalist," *Emerson Society Quarterly*, XXXIX, (1965), 28.
26. Conner, *Cosmic Optimism*, p. 86.
27. *Ibid.*, p. 176.
28. Elder, *Hawthorne, Transcendental Symbolist*, p. 40.
29. *Ibid.*, p. 87.
30. *Ibid.*, pp. 169–70.
31. *Ibid.*, p. 45.
32. Conner, p. 278.
33. *Ibid.*, p. 284.
34. Clark Griffith, *The Long Shadow: Emily Dickinson's Tragic Poetry* (Princeton, 1964), pp. 10–11.
35. *The Complete Poems of Emily Dickinson*, ed. Thomas H. Johnson (Boston, 1955). The numbering is Johnson's.
36. Glauco Cambon, "Emily Dickinson and the Crisis of Self-Reliance," in *Transcendentalism and Its Legacy*, pp. 123–32.
37. Marilyn Baldwin, "The Transcendental Phase of William Dean Howells," in Gittleman, *The Minor and Later Transcendentalists*, pp. 57–61.
38. In Gittleman, pp. 61–66.
39. *Robert Frost, Poetry and Prose*, ed. Edward C. Lathem and Lawrance Thompson (New York, 1972), p. 355.
40. Nina Baym, "The Transcendentalism of Wallace Stevens," in Gittleman, p. 67.
41. *Ibid.*
42. *Ibid.*, p. 69.
43. *Ibid.*, pp. 70–71.
44. *Literary History of the United States*, ed. Spiller *et al.*, 3rd ed. Rev. (New York, 1963), p. 1246.

45. Frederic I. Carpenter, "Eugene O'Neill, the Orient, and American Transcendentalism," in *Transcendentalism and Its Legacy*, p. 204.
46. *Ibid.*, p. 212.
47. *Ibid.*
48. Gittleman, p. 3.
49. Gay Wilson Allen, "James's *Varieties of Religious Experience* As Introduction to American Transcendentalism," *Emerson Society Quarterly*, XXXIX (1965), 81–85.
50. Emerson, *Journals*, VIII, 133.

Selected Bibliography

The following bibliography comprises books and articles either specifically referred to in the pages of this work or, in some instances, simply supportive in providing background information. Thus the list is by no means intended to be a comprehensive guide to material bearing on Transcendentalism in America; rather, it is selective and limited, for the most part, to those works that the author has found helpful in the preparation of this volume. Annotations are included for most items.

GENERAL WORKS

Brooks, Van Wyck. *The Flowering of New England*. New York: E.P. Dutton & Co., Inc., 1936.
    A very readable account of American thought and literature from 1815 to the Civil War, with vivid pen portraits of the leading Transcendentalists.
————. *New England: Indian Summer*. New York: E.P. Dutton & Co., Inc., 1940.
    From 1866 to 1915, with a good general account of the later phases of the Transcendental Movement.
Cook, Bruce. *The Beat Generation*. New York: Charles Scribner's Sons, 1971.
    Helpful in showing the influence of Transcendentalism on Beat poets like Ginsberg and Gary Snyder.
Curti, Merle. *The Growth of American Thought*. 3rd ed. revised. New York: Harper & Row, 1964.
    A good general discussion.
Ekirch, Arthur A. *The Idea of Progress in America, 1815–1860*. New York: Columbia University Press, 1944.
    Relates Transcendentalism to progressive thought.

Huber, Richard M. *The American Idea of Success*. New York: McGraw-Hill, 1971.
    A large-scale study of how the idea has permeated American life from the time of Franklin to the present.

Jones, Howard Mumford. "The Influence of European Ideas in Nineteenth-Century America," *American Literature* VII (1935), 241–73.

Jones, Rufus. *Studies in Mystical Religion.* London: Macmillan, 1909.

Matthiessen, F.O. *American Renaissance: Art and Expression in the Age of Emerson and Whitman.* New York: Oxford University Press, 1941.

    On the aesthetics of Emerson, Thoreau, Hawthorne, Melville and Whitman, with consideration of the Transcendental influence.

Meyer, Donald. *The Positive Thinkers.* Garden City, N.Y.: Doubleday & Co., Inc., 1965. Anchor Books paperback edition, 1966.

    A study of America's search for health, wealth, and power through "positive thinking" from Mary Baker Eddy to Norman Vincent Peale.

Miller, Perry, ed. *The American Transcendentalists: Their Prose and Poetry.* Garden City, N.Y.: Doubleday & Co., Inc., 1957.

    A convenient anthology of some of the literary achievements of the better known Transcendentalists.

———. *The Transcendentalists: An Anthology.* Cambridge, Mass.: Harvard University Press, 1950.

    The most complete anthology, ably edited with a sound general introduction and helpful introductions to individual selections.

Peel, Robert. *Christian Science. Its Encounter with American Culture.* New York: Holt, 1958.

    An enlightening account of Mrs. Eddy and her movement.

Schneider, Herbert W. *A History of American Philosophy.* 2nd ed. New York: Columbia University Press, 1963.

    Contains a good general view of Transcendental philosophy.

Spiller, Robert E. *et al.,* eds. *Literary History of the United States.* 3rd ed. New York: Macmillan, 1963.

    The bibliography on Transcendentalism is especially helpful.

Stovall, Floyd. *American Idealism.* Norman: University of Oklahoma Press, 1943.

    An interesting review of idealistic thought from the time of the Puritans.

Tanner, Tony. *The Reign of Wonder. Naivety and Reality in American Literature.* Cambridge: Cambridge University Press, 1965. Paperback edition by Harper & Row, New York, 1967.

    The first quarter of the book deals perceptively with the Transcendentalists and their point of view.

Whicher, George F., ed. *The Transcendentalist Revolt against Materialism.* Boston: D.C. Heath & Co., 1949.

    One of the Amherst College series of readings in American Studies.

SPECIAL STUDIES

Allen, Gay Wilson. "James's *Varieties of Religious Experience* As Intro-
duction to American Transcendentalism", *Emerson Society Quar-
terly* XXXIX (1965), 81-85.
   James's biographer explains why he thinks it to be the best book
to reveal what the Transcendentalists were talking and writing
about.
Anderson, Paul R. *Platonism in the Midwest.* New York and London: D.
Appleton-Century, 1963.
   A scholarly account of how the Platonic aspects of New England
Transcendentalism traveled west and took root there.
Buell, Lawrence. *Literary Transcendentalism: Style and Vision in the
American Renaissance.* Ithaca and London: Cornell University
Press, 1973.
   A comprehensive study of the Transcendentalist aesthetic, with
special attention to Emerson, Thoreau, Ellery Channing, Very,
and Whitman.
Carpenter, Frederic I. "American Transcendentalism in India, (1961),"
Emerson Society Quarterly XXXI (1963), 59–62.
   Produces interesting evidence of the impact on modern Indian
leaders of the thinking of Emerson and Thoreau.
Christy, Arthur E. *The Orient in American Transcendentalism: A Study
of Emerson, Thoreau, and Alcott.* New York: Columbia University
Press, 1932. Octagon Press published a 1963 reprint.
   This is a thorough study of the reading in Oriental literatures of
three prime participants in the Transcendental Movement.
Conner, Frederick W. *Cosmic Optimism.* Philadelphia: University of
Pennsylvania Press, 1949.
   A rewarding book that sees the Transcendentalist as establishing
his religious cosmology by denying that the mechanical categories
of science are more than superficially true and by showing that the
categories of purpose and value are more fundamental.
Frothingham, Octavius B. *Transcendentalism in New England.* New
York: G.P. Putnam's Sons, 1876. Harper Torchbook edition pub-
lished in 1959 with introduction by Sydney E. Ahlstrom.
   An invaluable history of the Transcendental Movement by one
who was involved. What it lacks in objectivity it gains in personal
knowledge of the subject.
Gittleman, Edwin, ed. *The Minor and Later Transcendentalists.*
Hartford, 1969.
   A symposium comprising twelve essays that are particularly use-
ful in establishing the modern connection.
Goddard, Harold C. *Studies in New England Transcendentalism.* New

York: Columbia University Press, 1908. A 1960 text edition has
been published by Hillary of New York.

 Particularly useful in tracing the background of the movement.
Channing, Emerson, Alcott, Parker, and Margaret Fuller are
studied in some detail.

Gohdes, Clarence L. F. *The Periodicals of American Transcendentalism.*
Durham: Duke University Press, 1931.

 The only thorough study of the subject.

Harmon, Frances B. *The Social Philosophy of the St. Louis Hegelians.*
New York: Columbia University Press, 1943.

 Centers on the lives and work of Henry C. Brokmeyer, William
Torrey Harris, and Denton J. Snider.

Hutchison, William R. *The Transcendental Ministers; Church Reform in
the New England Renaissance.* New Haven: Yale University Press,
1959. Reprinted by Shoe String Press, 1972.

 Scholarly treatment of the Unitarian background.

Kern, Alexander. "The Rise of Transcendentalism," in *Transitions in
American Literary History,* ed. Harry Hayden Clark. Durham:
Duke University Press, 1953.

 A good general survey.

Leighton, Walter L. *French Philosophers and New England Transcendentalism.* Charlottesville: University of Virginia Press, 1908. Reprint by Greenwood, 1968.

 A sound study of the French contribution, notably Victor
Cousin.

Pochmann, Henry A. *New England Transcendentalism and St. Louis
Hegelianism.* Philadelphia: Carl Schurz Memorial Foundation,
1948.

 Shows the relations between New England Transcendentalism
and the St. Louis Movement in philosophy, literature, and education, as well as the interactions in education between the St. Louis
group and the Concord School of Philosophy.

Porte, Joel. *Emerson and Thoreau: Transcendentalists in Conflict.*
Middletown, Conn.: Wesleyan University Press, 1965.

 A study that views the difference between the transcendentalism
of Emerson and Thoreau as the intellectual vs. the sensuous, and
which sees both as necessary to an adequate definition of Transcendentalism.

Sams, Henry W., ed. *Autobiography of Brook Farm.* Englewood Cliffs,
N.J.: Prentice-Hall, Inc., 1958.

 An excellent collection of materials for reconstructing the story
of a noble experiment.

Simon, Myron and Thornton H. Parsons, eds. *Transcendentalism and Its
Legacy.* Ann Arbor: University of Michigan Press, 1966.

An excellent collection of essays illustrating the influence of Transcendentalism.

Swift, Lindsay. *Brook Farm, Its Members, Scholars, and Visitors.* New York: Macmillan, 1900.

An indispensable record.

Washburn, Wilcomb E. "The Orient in Mid-Nineteenth Century American Literature," *The Southwestern Journal* V, no. 1 (1950).

———. "The Oriental 'Roots' of American Transcendentalism," *The Southwestern Journal*, IV, 4 (1949).

Valuable discussions of the Oriental influence, contending that the New England Transcendentalists failed to grasp the ideas of the Oriental scriptures.

Wellek, René. "The Minor Transcendentalists and German Philosophy," *New England Quarterly* XV, no. 4 (Dec. 1942), 652–80.

Particularly interesting in showing Bronson Alcott as unfavorable to Kant, whose philosophy he viewed as pedestrian and sensual.

Wells, Ronald V. *Three Christian Transcendentalists.* New York: Columbia University Press, 1943. Reprinted by Octagon, 1972, with new MS material and a new introduction.

Treats authoritatively of the lives and views of Frederic Henry Hedge, James Marsh, and Caleb Sprague Henry.

Williams, Paul O. *The Transcendental Movement in American Poetry.* Ph.D. dissertation, University of Pennsylvania, 1962.

A sensitive treatment of an important aspect of the movement. Sees Emerson, Thoreau, and Very as the most successful of the Transcendentalist poets.

INDIVIDUAL AUTHORS

A. Bronson Alcott

The Journals of Bronson Alcott. Edited by Odell Shepard. Boston: Little, Brown & Co., 1938.

Sears, Clara E. *Bronson Alcott's Fruitlands.* Boston: Houghton, Mifflin Co., 1915.

Shepard, Odell. *Pedlar's Progress: The Life of Bronson Alcott.* Boston: Little, Brown & Co., 1937.

An excellent biography.

Orestes A. Brownson

The Works of Orestes A. Brownson. Edited by Henry F. Brownson, 20 vols. Detroit: Nourse, 1882–1907.

Maynard, Theodore. *Orestes Brownson: Yankee, Radical, Catholic.* New York: Macmillan, 1943.

A very useful biography, with extensive bibliography.

William Ellery Channing

Brown, Arthur W. *Always Young for Liberty*. Syracuse: Syracuse University Press, 1956.

> The best biography to date.

——. *William Ellery Channing*. New York: Twayne, 1961. Revised and enlarged.

Christopher Pearse Cranch

Miller, F. DeWolfe. *Christopher Pearse Cranch and His Caricatures of New England Transcendentalism*. Cambridge: Harvard University Press, 1951.

> Reproduces many of the delightful Cranch drawings.

Scott, Leonora Cranch. *The Life and Letters of Christopher Pearse Cranch*. Boston: Houghton Mifflin Co., 1917. Reprinted, New York: AMS Press, 1969.

> The only attempt at a complete biography.

John Sullivan Dwight

Fertig, Walter L. *John Sullivan Dwight: transcendentalist and literary amateur of music*. College Park, Md.: University of Maryland dissertation in typescript, 1952.

> More informative than George W. Cooke's 1898 biography, but unfortunately not in print.

Ralph Waldo Emerson

The Complete Works of Ralph Waldo Emerson. Edited by Edward Waldo Emerson. 12 vols. Boston: Houghton, Mifflin Co., 1903–06.

The Journals and Miscellaneous Notebooks. Edited by William H. Gilman *et al.* 10 vols. to date. Cambridge, Mass.: Belknap Press of Harvard University Press, 1960–.

> An indispensable tool for the study of Emerson, it will, when complete, supplant the Emerson-Forbes *Journals of Ralph Waldo Emerson* of 1909–1914.

The Letters of Ralph Waldo Emerson. Edited by Ralph L. Rusk. 6 vols. New York: Columbia University Press, 1939.

Selected Prose and Poetry. 2nd ed. Edited by Reginald L. Cook. New York: Holt, Rinehart and Winston, 1969.

> An intelligent selection, especially good on poetry.

The Selected Writings of Ralph Waldo Emerson. Edited by Brooks Atkinson. New York: Modern Library, 1950.

> The most complete one-volume anthology of Emerson's work.

Anderson, John Q. *The Liberating Gods; Emerson on Poets and Poetry*. Coral Gables, Fla.: University of Miami Press, 1971.

A close and imaginative examination of Emerson's aesthetics, offering particularly valuable insights to "The Poet."

Bishop, Jonathan. *Emerson on the Soul.* Cambridge, Mass.: Harvard University Press, 1964.

An extended analysis of the meanings of Emerson's transcendentalism.

Cameron, Kenneth Walter. *Emerson the Essayist.* 2 vols. Raleigh, N.C.: Thistle Press, 1945.

Attempts to establish Coleridge as preeminent among the teachers of Emerson.

————. *Young Emerson's Transcendental Vision; an exposition of his world view with an analysis of the structure, backgrounds, and meaning of Nature* (1836). Hartford, 1971.

Carpenter, Frederic Ives. *Emerson and Asia.* Cambridge, Mass.: Harvard University Press, 1930.

A thorough examination of Emerson's reading in Oriental literatures.

————. *Emerson Handbook.* New York: Hendricks House, 1953.

A mine of ready information.

Harrison, John S. *The Teachers of Emerson.* New York: Sturgis and Walton, 1910.

A thorough discussion of the Platonic and Neoplatonic influence.

Konvitz, Milton, and Stephen Whicher, eds. *Emerson: A Collection of Critical Essays.* Englewood Cliffs, N.J.: Prentice-Hall, 1962.

An excellent selection, with a good introduction by Konvitz.

Nicoloff, Philip L. *Emerson on Race and History.* New York: Columbia University Press, 1961.

Sees Carlyle's influence as much less than is usually suggested, with Neoplatonism more important.

Paul, Sherman. *Emerson's Angle of Vision.* Cambridge, Mass.: Harvard University Press, 1952.

Studies Emerson's idea of "correspondence" and the part it played in his thought.

Rusk, Ralph L. *The Life of Ralph Waldo Emerson.* New York: Charles Scribner's Sons, 1949.

The indispensable biography.

Slater, Joseph, ed. *The Correspondence of Emerson and Carlyle.* New York: Columbia University Press, 1964.

An excellent collection of the voluminous correspondence with a good introduction and helpful annotation.

Stovall, Floyd, ed. *Eight American Authors.* New York: Modern Language Association, 1956.

Includes an excellent chapter on Emerson by the editor.

Whicher, Stephen. *Freedom and Fate; An Inner Life of Ralph Waldo Emerson.* Philadelphia: University of Pennsylvania Press, 1953.

An extremely able and imaginative study of Emerson's ideas and writings.

Margaret Fuller

The Writings of Margaret Fuller, edited by Mason Wade. New York: Viking, 1941.

An ample selection, with a good bibliography of the published writings.

Brown, Arthur W. *Margaret Fuller*. New York: Twayne, 1964.

The most up-to-date biography.

Wade, Mason. *Margaret Fuller: Whetstone of Genius*. New York: Viking, 1940.

The life story by the editor of her writings.

Nathaniel Hawthorne

The Heart of Hawthorne's Journals. Edited by Newton Arvin. Boston: Houghton, Mifflin Co., 1929.

Contains in a convenient single volume Hawthorne's journal comments on Transcendentalism.

Elder, Marjorie J. *Nathaniel Hawthorne, Transcendental Symbolist*. Athens, Ohio: Ohio University Press, 1969.

An excellent study of the Transcendentalist aesthetic as manifested in Hawthorne's work.

Theodore Parker

The Works of Theodore Parker. 15 vols. Boston: American Unitarian Association, 1907–1913.

Commager, Henry Steele. *Theodore Parker*. Boston: Little, Brown, 1936.

An extremely readable and enthusiastic biography by an eminent historian.

Weiss, John. *Life and Correspondence of Theodore Parker*. 2 vols. New York: D. Appleton & Co., 1864.

By a minor Transcendentalist, this is valuable particularly for the correspondence.

George Ripley

Frothingham, Octavius B. *George Ripley*. New York: AMS Press, 1970.

Reprint of the 1883 edition.

Still the best account of the founder of Brook Farm.

Henry David Thoreau

Collected Poems of Henry Thoreau, edited by Carl Bode. Baltimore: Johns Hopkins University Press, 1964.

The Correspondence of Henry David Thoreau, edited by Walter Harding and Carl Bode. New York: New York University Press, 1958.

The Writings of Henry David Thoreau. 20 vols. Boston: Houghton, Mifflin Co., 1906.

The standard edition, including fourteen volumes of the journal.

Bode, Carl, ed. *The Best of Thoreau's Journals.* Carbondale and Edwardsville, Ill.: Southern Illinois University Press, 1967.

An excellent selection with a very useful foreword by the editor.

——. *The Portable Thoreau.* New York: Viking Press, 1947. Rev. 1964.

The best convenient anthology.

Harding, Walter. *A Thoreau Handbook.* New York: New York University Press, 1959.

Summarizes and evaluates Thoreau scholarship.

——. *The Days of Henry Thoreau.* New York: Alfred A. Knopf, 1965.

The most complete and scholarly biography.

Krutch, Joseph Wood. *Henry David Thoreau.* New York: Sloane, 1948.

An excellent appreciation of Thoreau's ideas.

Shanley, James L. *The Making of Walden.* Chicago: University of Chicago Press, 1957.

A detailed and valuable study of the way in which Thoreau's masterpiece was composed.

Jones Very

Poems and Essays. Edited by James Freeman Clarke. Boston: Houghton Mifflin Co., 1886.

Bartlett, William Irving. *Jones Very: Emerson's "Brave Saint."* Durham, N.C.: Duke University Press, 1942.

Contains many helpful critical comments as well as the life story.

Gittleman, Edwin. *Jones Very: The Effective Years.* New York: Columbia University Press, 1967.

Concentrates on Very's productive period.

Walt Whitman

The Complete Writings of Walt Whitman. 10 vols. Edited by Richard M. Bucke, Thomas B. Harned, and Horace L. Traubel. New York: G. P. Putnam's Sons, 1902.

Leaves of Grass. Edited by Sculley Bradley and Harold W. Blodgett. New York: New York University Press, 1965. Reprint, Norton, 1973.

The most complete collection of Whitman's work in one volume. Besides the poems, there is a section on "Whitman on His Art" as well as a wide range of criticism.

Allen, Gay Wilson. *The Solitary Singer.* New York: Macmillan, 1955.

The definitive biography.

Index